Freedom from Hijacked Emotions

Overcoming Anxiety, Anger, and Fear

Dr. Randy Carlson

IntentionalLiving PRESS

Freedom from Hijacked Emotions: Overcoming Anxiety, Anger, and Fear
Dr. Randy Carlson
© 2019 by Dr. Randy Carlson. All rights reserved.

Editing by Adam Colwell's WriteWorks, LLC, Adam Colwell and Ginger Colwell
Cover design by Jimmy Anaya
Typesetting by Inktobook.com
Published by Intentional Living Press
Printed in the United States of America
ISBN (Paperback): 978-1-7341458-0-9
ISBN (eBook): 978-1-7341458-1-6

All Scripture quotations, unless otherwise marked, are taken from THE HOLY BIBLE, NEW INTERNATIONAL VERSION®. Copyright© 1973, 1978, 1984, 2011 by Biblica, Inc.™. Used by permission of Zondervan.
Other Bible versions used are:
Scripture quotations marked (TM) are taken from the THE MESSAGE: THE BIBLE IN
CONTEMPORARY ENGLISH, copyright© 1993, 1994, 1995, 1996, 2000, 2001, 2002. Used by permission of NavPress Publishing Group.
Scripture quotations marked (NKJV) are taken from the NEW KING JAMES VERSION®.
Copyright© 1982 by Thomas Nelson, Inc. Used by permission. All rights reserved.
Scripture quotations marked (KJV) are taken from the KING JAMES VERSION, public domain.
Scripture quotations marked (NLT) are taken from the HOLY BIBLE, NEW LIVING TRANSLATION, Copyright© 1996, 2004, 2007 by Tyndale House Foundation. Used by

permission of Tyndale House Publishers, Inc., Carol Stream, Illinois 60188. All rights reserved. Used by permission.

All rights reserved. Except in the case of brief quotations embodied in critical articles and reviews, no portion of this book may be reproduced, stored in a retrieval system, or transmitted in any form or by any means—electronic, mechanical, photocopy, recording, scanning, or other—without the prior written permission from the author. None of the material in this book may be reproduced for any commercial promotion, advertising or sale of a product or service.

Dedication

To my beautiful wife, Donna. Thank you for loving me even during those times when a hijacked emotion gets the better part of my day.

Acknowledgments

The writing of *Freedom from Hijacked Emotions* started several years ago from observations that strong healthy relationships require emotionally mature people. There are no emotional shortcuts to healthy relationships! Hijacked emotions are front and center pain points in most counseling offices. This led me to write an early draft of this book. That early draft sat on the bookshelf in my office waiting for me to get intentional. Without the encouragement and assistance of several people near to me, I fear that early draft would still be in that notebook.

We teach at the Intentional Living Center© that success starts with a decision and becomes a reality through daily action. That's a fact! So, once I decided the time was *now* to finish this project, things started to come together. After many months of hard work, the book you hold in your hands became a reality.

Like most worthwhile projects, success requires the

dedication and hard work of a lot of people with different gifts. That was true with this book. So, let me first thank my editor, Adam Colwell, for your excellent blend of editing and writing creativity, and for the management of detail that you brought to this project. Adam, you helped to sharpen my thoughts and helped me craft my words for the benefit of the reader. I also want to express my appreciation to Shanna Gregor, Jim Ray, and Dawn Heitger, each of whom contributed in some way to that earliest draft of the book.

I also want to extend my thanks to my staff who took the time to read drafts of the manuscript and for providing excellent feedback. I want to especially thank my executive assistant, Cindie Conley; senior radio and podcast producer, Rob Regal; radio producer, Steven Davis; our ministry's creative services director, Taylor Anderson; chief engagement officer, Sally Barton; and my sister-in-law Cheri Carlson for your help and support. I also want to add a special thanks to our graphic artist, Jimmy Anaya, for creating the outstanding cover for the book. Well done, Jimmy!

I'm also grateful to my radio and podcast listeners for providing motivation for this book. Each story in *Freedom from Hijacked Emotions* is a composite from the many stories I've heard over the years from listeners and conference attendees. While the stories I shared about myself are as they really happened in my life, the stories of others have been significantly altered to protect the identity of any person.

Finally, I want to acknowledge my wife, Donna. Without your love and support, neither this book, nor any

Acknowledgments

of my other books, would have been possible. Your willingness to allow me time away to work on this book, and your patience as you carefully read through the numerous drafts, was invaluable. Donna, you are the love of my life.

Table of Contents

YOU CAN LIVE FREE! — xiii

CHAPTER ONE — 1
Being Intentional When Emotions Become a Problem

CHAPTER TWO — 21
The Emotional Languages of Head, Heart, and Hand

CHAPTER THREE — 39
Tell Yourself the Truth

CHAPTER FOUR — 59
Taming Anger: The Explosive Hijacker

CHAPTER FIVE — 81
Tearing Down the Walls of Anxiety and Fear

CHAPTER SIX — 101
How to Get Through an Emotional Dip

CHAPTER SEVEN 127
When Words Boil Over

CHAPTER EIGHT 149
Intentionally Go Forward Toward Freedom

ONE MORE THING 167

APPENDIX 171

You Can Live Free!

None of us are ever very far away from allowing our emotions to hijack our lives. Hijacked emotions have destroyed marriages, estranged families, destroyed relationships, ruined people's health, and forced people into bankruptcy. Some have lost their jobs as their emotions consumed them. Maybe you picked up this book feeling like your life is on hold—you're not advancing in your career, your finances are a mess, or you feel ineffective as a parent—because your emotions have been hijacked.

It's vital to understand and manage your emotions. After all, your emotions are the window to your soul. If I could look into your eyes and observe your behavior for just a few minutes, I could get an idea of where you are emotionally. I might be clueless about what's going on in your head, but your emotions show on your face. We can pick up where we are emotionally through nonverbal clues.

The truth is, your success in life depends upon how well you recognize and deal with your emotions. *Freedom*

Freedom from Hijacked Emotions

from Hijacked Emotions will unveil the secret of making **five bold moves** that will change your life and help you manage any negative emotions. They are:

Bold Move 1: DECIDE who's in charge of your emotions. Your emotions are yours. Therefore, you can redirect them from negative to positive outcomes. The problem isn't anger, fear, guilt, or any other negative emotion. They are common to life. It's what you do with them that matters. Instead of doing something dumb (sinful), you can learn to use that emotion as fuel to propel you toward a healthy response. The power to take ownership of your emotions comes from God. His love will give you the courage to retain that ownership, and a sound mind will enable you to manage your emotions for God's glory and your benefit (2 Timothy 1:7).

Bold Move 2: DECLARE who's in charge of your emotions. This solidifies your decision to take ownership of your emotions. Using the emotion of fear as an example, tell it, "Fear, I feel you, but you are not in charge. I will not be controlled by you!" The more often you declare the truth, the more it will stick in your life. As my life verse, Philippians 4:8, proclaims, "Whatever is true, whatever is noble, whatever is right, whatever is pure, whatever is lovely, whatever is admirable—if anything is excellent or praiseworthy—think about such things." It reminds me that I'm responsible to take control of my thoughts, for it is our thinking that drives how we respond to our emotions.

You Can Live Free!

Bold Move 3: DEVELOP a plan of action to respond to emotional triggers. You cannot wait to do this. Your good intention will not be enough to prevent your emotions from being hijacked. One of my emotional triggers is getting cut off in traffic. My emotional desire at that moment is to speed up and engage by allowing thoughts that are aggressive and combative as a way to retaliate. But my bold move is to actually slow down, assume the other driver had a reason to do what they did, focus on where I'm headed, and stay away from engaging improper thoughts. This has helped reduce my stress while driving in busy traffic and probably kept me out of trouble with other drivers.

Bold Move 4: DECLUTTER your emotions, leaving margin for bad days. At our Intentional Living Center, we teach people to declutter their lives in other areas: mental, financial, relational, and work. Too much clutter in each of these essential areas typically adds to our emotional challenges.

Bold Move 5: DO the next right one thing, protecting your emotions from getting hijacked. In my book, *The Power of One Thing – How to Intentionally Change Your Life*, I wrote:

One thing done once is an experience.
One thing done twice has your attention.
One thing done often is a pursuit.
One thing done always is a habit.[1]

I will reinforce how each one of these **five bold moves** will keep your emotions from getting hijacked, taking your peace captive in the process. Throughout the book, I'll share several "Make a Bold Move" tips and end each chapter with questions tied to those tips. Both are designed to equip you to apply *Intentional Living*® principles to your emotional life.

Join me now as we journey together and discover how to live free from hijacked emotions.

1

Being Intentional When Emotions Become a Problem

Living an intentional life is about making decisions and then intentionally managing those decisions for God's glory and for the benefit of yourself and those around you. Managing emotions is essential to that process. Having an emotional response to something is normal. Hijacking occurs when your emotions become the cause of the problem instead of the fuel to solve the problem.

Every day, you maneuver your way through a veritable minefield of emotionally-laden triggers. It could be getting cut off in traffic, hearing unthoughtful words from your spouse, the rolling eyes of your teenager, a long line at the bank, or a bad report from your doctor. Each one of these daily experiences is interpreted through the lenses of expectation and intention. I judge myself by my intention, but I judge others by my expectations—and they judge me the same way. Since we believe our intentions are good, then we feel an unmet expectation must be someone else's fault.

A caller to my nationally-syndicated radio show, *Intentional Living*, once shared, "I've asked my husband a thousand times to hang up his clothes and not just leave them on a chair or on the floor of the closet. It makes me angry. It makes me withdraw. He wonders what the problem is, and I end up getting my emotions hijacked in the process, over something that is actually really stupid." It's easy to do. Whether it's a relatively minor issue such as dirty laundry or a major conflict, whenever an expectation exceeds reality, the result will always be disappointment, which can easily lead to a hijacked emotion. I suggested that she tell her husband that she is not his maid, and if he leaves his clothes on the floor, she will simply leave them there or throw them in a nearby box for him to take care of later. In my book *Starved for Affection*, I call that response "active respect."[1] It's where you show a person you love and respect them enough to hold them accountable for their behavior with natural and logical consequences. Active respect is Bible-based: "Do not be deceived: God cannot be mocked. A man reaps what he sows." (Galatians 6:7) It's where we don't let people get away with poor behavior just because we love them.

> **I judge myself by my intention, but I judge others by my expectations.**

Emotions are the human fuel that either moves you to change, grow, and learn, or they cause you to smolder,

Being Intentional When Emotions Become a Problem

explode, and poison your life and the lives of those around you.

Make a Bold Move: DECLARE who's in charge of your emotions.

1. Whenever you declare who's in charge of your emotions by saying, "I'm responsible for my emotions with God's help," you take back control of your emotions and keep them from being hijacked.
2. Be prepared with a healthy response the next time someone lights up your emotional fuse. Preparation is one of the most important steps in intentionally taking back control of hijacked emotions.
3. Stay emotionally positive in the face of negative people. You can do this by not taking things personally or feeling you always need to correct or defend a position.

THE IMPACT OF TRAUMA

When you experience great loss, it can easily overwhelm you emotionally. When your world gets rocked, it's very stressful. Soldiers routinely return from combat duty with post-traumatic stress disorder (PTSD), which can also be caused by other events such as a sexual assault, an unexpected death, or a natural disaster. Emergency workers who are exposed to tragedy can also develop PTSD. People get traumatized by something, and it really plays with their emotions in their life. I remember one young man who came back from the Iraq war. He was dropped on the battlefield when he was 18, fresh out of basic training. What he saw and experienced changed his life, and the results of his trauma deeply impacted his marriage through anger and withdrawing from his spouse and other people. There are times when our emotions have been so damaged that we need professional help from a counselor or psychologist to help us deal with it.

Trauma can reach back as far as our earliest childhood memories. I was conducting an early childhood memory conference to a sold-out crowd in California, teaching from my book, *Unlocking the Secrets of Your Childhood Memories*. One person recalled many childhood memories of her father and mother arguing and fighting. "All I wanted was for them to stop and for our home to be calm," she said. As she shared the memory, she became just like that little girl all over again. You could almost see her trying to stand between her mom and dad and separate them, even though they weren't actually in the room with her. After revealing her powerful, hurtful memories of growing up in an angry home, I asked how that affected her today. "I need to control everything," she said. "Even when I'm baking

> **Here's a fact: children are excellent observers of our behavior, but terrible interpreters of adult issues and conflict.**

an apple pie, if the crust is not perfect, I will throw the whole thing away and start over."

Because she felt controlling her world was vital to her safety, her marriage was negatively impacted by her perfectionism, and her unreasonable expectations for her children caused them to resent her constant criticism.

How we remember our childhood, the words that we use, and the emotions we attach to them reflects more about who we are today than the story itself. In my book, *Father Memories*, I wrote, "Fathers leave a lasting impression on the lives of their children. Picture fathers all around the world carving their initials into their family trees. Like a carving in the trunk of an oak, as time passes the impressions fathers make on their children grow deeper and wider. Depending upon how the tree grows, those impressions can either be ones of harmony or ones of distortion."[2] Here's a fact: children are excellent observers of our behavior, but terrible interpreters of adult issues and conflict. There are things that are better dealt with behind closed doors.

Make a Bold Move: DECLUTTER your emotions.

1. Your early recollections are like a picture of how you see life today. Don't be surprised when you discover your emotions, or lack of emotions, from early childhood memories are similar to your emotions, or lack of emotions, today. That's how God wired us.
2. Don't allow your childhood memories to keep you trapped. Instead of "forgiving"

and "forgetting," try "forgiving" and "remembering" all that God has done in forgiving you.
3. Ask your siblings about their childhood memories. You may be surprised how their memories and emotions from childhood are very different than yours. That's because you're different people, and we tend to remember things from our childhood in ways that are consistent with how we view life today.

Emotion always creates a reaction, and all emotion has a point of origin. In the word "emotion," the prefix "e" means *coming out from*. The word "motion" means *movement*. So, our emotions are a result of something that happens to us. Emotions have their own laws of physics. Emotions create movement in our lives. Positive or negative, every emotion you experience has an equal or opposite reaction.

EXPLOSIVE AND SMOLDERING EMOTIONS

My wife and I live in the Arizona desert. Sagebrush and tall dry grass surround our house. One hot summer day, I saw smoke billowing in the air just outside the wall of our backyard. Within minutes, it had transformed into an aggressive brush fire. Knowing immediate action was required before things got worse and my home was threatened, I called the fire department. The blaze was extinguished with no damage to our property, but the charred grass was a vivid reminder how quickly that fire grew and became dangerous.

Hijacked emotions can burn like a fire within your soul, starting with a small spark that can rapidly swell into a large blaze. A healthy response will douse the emotions before they can do any damage, but an unhealthy reaction can be destructive. You're not alone if you struggle with the stressful and painful results of hijacked emotions. It's a worldwide problem. Did you know…

- Americans are among the most stressed people in the world. In fact, the United States has one of the highest rates out of the 143 countries studied, and it beat the global average by a full 20 percentage points. The U.S. ties statistically with Greece, which has led the world on this measure every year since 2012.
- Nearly half (45 percent) felt worried a lot.
- More than one in five (22 percent) felt angry a lot.
- Younger Americans between the ages of 15-49 are among the most stressed, worried, and angry in the U.S. Roughly two in three of those younger than 50 said they experienced stress a lot, about half said they felt worried a lot, and at least one in four or more felt anger a lot.
- The world in general took a negative turn in 2017, with global levels of stress, worry, sadness, and pain hitting new highs.[3]

Each one of these statistics is the result of hijacked emotion that moves from a simple stress reaction to a destructive explosive reaction. When this happens, these explosive people can be very controlling. They say and do things that warn people to stay away and not get too close. If you are an emotionally explosive person, you need to remember there are warning lights within your heart that will begin to blink before the eruption ever occurs, telling you something is not quite right. You're not the only one seeing that warning light, either. I don't have to be around someone very long to discern that their emotional state is about to spin out of control.

> **When you bury your emotions, you bury them *alive*.**

Hijacked emotions can smolder within you as well. Feelings of bitterness, resentment, or unforgiveness will quietly burn until they inflict a wound that can do deep emotional damage to your soul. When you bury your emotions, you bury them *alive*. You may think you've snuffed them out, but they're still smoldering, and they're not going anywhere. Eventually, you have to deal with those feelings to truly put them out.

Let's say you have issues with your siblings or your parents. Maybe no one talks about what happened to create those issues, but you remember every moment. This often comes up as families settle the estate of their parents. For example, mom survives dad's death. When she passes, she leaves everything behind. Sometimes the estate is clear, but most of the time it is not. Little things, like who gets to take mom's trinkets, bring out lingering issues of disappointment or resentment—and these little things become big things. Their hijacked emotions lead to years of estrangement that sometimes last for a lifetime.

Often, something inside your heart needs to be resolved. Your hijacked emotions have tugged and dragged your feelings down, leaving you at risk of doing damage to yourself, those you love, and possibly even those you hardly know. The signs might not be as obvious as they are for the explosive person, but they're there, and the resulting damage is just as real.

WARNING SIGNS

Any time your emotions negatively interfere with any one of the five essential areas of your life—faith, relationships, health, finances, and work—you should be concerned. Here are 10 warning signs that a hijacked emotion is an issue in your life:

1. When compulsive behavior is a problem: overspending, overeating, over-anything.
2. When you're constantly feeling overwhelmed as a parent.
3. When your emotions have cost you a job or friendship.
4. When you consistently withdraw from people for no apparent reason.
5. When your physician tells you your physical symptoms aren't originating from a physical problem.
6. When others feel like they need to walk on eggshells around you.

7. When road rage is a regular problem.
8. When you often feel loneliness or some other emotion for no apparent reason.
9. When you've developed nervous habits you didn't use to exhibit.
10. When you're unhappy more than ever before.

Make a Bold Move: DO the next right one thing.

1. Don't ignore emotional warning signs. Ask a trusted friend or family member to honestly share what they've observed about your emotional reactions.
2. Become mindful of the emotional roots of your hijacked emotions. Treating the roots will take care of the rest.
3. Ask God to reveal to you any negative behavior in your life that is controlled by a hijacked emotion.

Based on talking with thousands of people both on and off the air, I've concluded that upwards of 90 percent of those marriages that fail did so because somebody's emotions were hijacked. I've witnessed loneliness leading to affairs, anger leading to abuse, guilt leading to depression, and fear leading to controlling behavior—and each can lead to divorce.

The same can be said for those who fail in the workplace. Because of hijacked emotions, they can't get along with people, can't relate, and can't resolve problems. One man who called in to my radio show and podcast wanted

Being Intentional When Emotions Become a Problem

to know if I thought it was okay for him to move his whole family closer to where his wife's family lived in South Dakota.

I told him, "That sounds reasonable. Why do you ask?"

He then revealed he had been through seven jobs in two years and had been fired each time—and thought it would be nice to be close to them for support.

I told him he was asking the wrong question. The question he should ask himself is, "Why have I been fired seven times in two years?" The right question at the right time to the right person can change your life.

I've also observed that the vast majority of parents with hijacked emotions feel overwhelmed, often leading to overreacting out of frustration and anger. Perhaps they experience fear and don't act in the best interest of their children because they're afraid they'll overreact. In my conferences, I teach a concept called "parent up and power down," a principle from my longtime teachings about raising responsible adults. It says to parent up, do the next right one thing, have a plan, and do it as a team if you are married, but power down your emotions in the process so that you will make good decisions and protect your relationship with your kids. This simple formula has helped thousands of parents to get a handle on their emotional response to parenting.

> **The right question at the right time to the right person can change your life.**

There's no doubt. When your emotions hijack your life,

you're dead when it comes to relationships—and what is life without relationships? Raul was a Christian that grew up in church. He was involved in leadership, singing in the choir, and was part of the men's group. His life was in order. Things were moving well, and he didn't seem to have any problems. Yet he mistook activity for satisfaction in his marriage, and in the midst of all the things he was doing, he was missing his wife's heart. She was drawn into an affair, and as a result, his world was shattered.

Raul fell into a depression that turned into anger toward his wife expressed through the hurtful things he said and the games that were played in trying to determine custody of their children during their divorce proceedings. He then became disillusioned and rejected God and his faith. That affected his health because he stopped taking care of himself even though he was a diabetic. Things got so out of control, Raul ended up in the hospital with severe foot problems. All of this started to negatively impact his job, and he stopped using good judgment with money. He bought a new car thinking it was going to make him feel better, but it didn't. The financial obligation only added more stress. In the divorce proceedings, Raul ended up having some of his wages garnished, and he eventually lost his job.

This tale of woe shows how the five essential areas of life are interrelated and influenced by hijacked emotions. His faith, health, finances, and work were all adversely impacted as his most important relationship fell apart. I wish I could tell you how his story turned out. I don't know the outcome. But I do know our outcomes will be

Being Intentional When Emotions Become a Problem

bad unless we manage our emotions and keep them from being hijacked when things go wrong.

Here are some other ways each of the five essential areas of life can be negatively influenced by your hijacked emotions:

- Faith: Disappointment and doubt about your circumstances can become so strong, you can question the validity of everything you believe about God and His Word. You ask yourself, "Why does God allow bad things to happen to good people of faith when I see so many people who reject God and faith prospering?" Counter this wrong thinking by trusting God and staying connected to Him by praying, reading Scripture, and staying engaged in your church (Psalm 42:5).
- Relationships: Discord in your marriage can cause emotions to heat up in the wrong way, resulting in negative words and actions. When this happens, stay focused on doing the next right one thing in your relationship. Encourage every day. Forgive every day. Develop shared goals (Colossians 3:13).
- Health: Stress can cause ulcers and fluctuations in your blood pressure. You can also experience fatigue, anxiety, or crave comfort food, all of which can create medical problems. People smoke or look to drugs to ease the discomfort brought by hijacked emotions. Respond by learning to relax, meditating on Scripture, eating healthy, and exercising (Psalm 46:10).
- Finances: Two extremes are possible. It can be

overspending from a little too much "retail therapy" at the outlet mall, or it can be hoarding by holding on to money or things because you're afraid to be without either one. Spending or hoarding are unhealthy emotional outlets. Take control by creating a budget and sticking with it. Use money. Don't be used by it (Matthew 6:24).
- Work: I've seen people experience a lack of focus at work or allow hijacked emotions to lead to miscommunication with coworkers. Feelings of unproductiveness or the reaction to procrastinate are also common. Remember that we judge ourselves by our intentions, but others judge us by their expectations. Your coworkers expect to have an emotionally safe place to work. Intentionally strive to meet that expectation (Colossians 3:17).

CHANGING MINDSETS

If your emotional reactions are keeping you from being successful in any of the five essential areas, why settle for an incomplete life? It's time to become intentional and act. It's time to change and begin successfully managing your emotions.

Thoughts drive our emotions, and our emotions drive our actions. No wonder the Bible tells us that as a man "thinks in his heart, so is he." (Proverbs 23:7, NKJV) Have you ever referred to someone as being "narrow minded," "open minded," or "closed minded?" These types of mindsets play into our emotional lives.

The mindset of "I'll do it later" originates from fear and leads to procrastination.

The mindset of "I can't do it" originates from insecurity and leads to fear.

The mindset of "I don't need other people" originates from pride and leads to self-protection.

The mindset of "I have the right to be angry" originates from control and leads to blaming others.

The mindset of "I can't forgive them" originates from anger and leads to unforgiveness and bitterness.

To avoid hijacked emotions, you will need to identify unhealthy mindsets and seek God's help in changing them. Romans 12:2 gives you a great place to start. It says, "Do not conform to the pattern of this world, but be transformed by the renewing of your mind. Then you will be able to test and approve what God's will is—his good, pleasing and perfect will."

A change in your actions can also have positive emotional responses. If you're feeling down, for example, get up and go for a walk. Start reading the Bible regularly. Sometimes you just have to say to yourself, *Hey, I don't feel like it, but I'm going to do it anyway.* With just a little bit of action, you'll start to feel better.

The most effective thing you can do to successfully manage your emotions is to choose to think and behave like Christ. This principle is supported throughout Scripture, but one of my favorite passages is Philippians 4:6. "Do not be anxious about anything, but in every situation, by prayer and petition, with thanksgiving, present your requests to God." The Apostle Paul gives clear instruction that is action-oriented. He's saying, "Do these things." He's not suggesting you have to feel anything at this point. Just do something. What is the result? "And the peace of God, which transcends all understanding, will guard your hearts and your minds in Christ Jesus." (Philippians 4:7)

JOSEPH'S EXAMPLE

There's a great account in the Bible of a man who, even before Jesus' time on earth, thought and behaved like Christ. His name was Joseph, and it's well worth your time to read his entire story in Genesis 37-50. He was emotionally and physically abused by his brothers, sold into slavery, wrongfully accused by his employer, and cast into prison. Joseph had every reason to experience a myriad of hijacked emotions, but he had an amazing attitude. He maintained his composure. He didn't lose it. He didn't let his emotions get the best of him. He stayed the course and did the next right one thing. Later in life, during seven years of harvest, Joseph was brought to a place of authority in Egypt where he intentionally prepared the people for an upcoming famine after being warned about it by God. When his brothers started running out of food, they came to him, not recognizing who he was. But Joseph knew his brothers. How could he possibly forget those who betrayed him?

Can you imagine what he could have been thinking? *Wow, I've got them now. Whatever goes around, comes*

Being Intentional When Emotions Become a Problem

around. But Joseph did not allow his emotions to be hijacked by hatred or unforgiveness. "Joseph said to his brothers, 'Come close to me.' When they had done so, he said, 'I am your brother Joseph, the one you sold into Egypt! And now, do not be distressed and do not be angry with yourselves for selling me here, because it was to save lives that God sent me ahead of you.'" (Genesis 45:4-5) What perspective! What mercy! He continued: "For two years now there has been famine in the land, and for the next five years there will be no plowing and reaping. But God sent me ahead of you to preserve for you a remnant on earth and to save your lives by a great deliverance." (Genesis 45:6-7)

Joseph was clearly thinking and behaving like Christ, causing him to later proclaim, "'Don't be afraid. Am I in the place of God? You intended to harm me, but God intended it for good to accomplish what is now being done, the saving of many lives. So then, don't be afraid. I will provide for you and your children.' And he reassured them and spoke kindly to them." (Genesis 50:19-21) Joseph knew God's intentions and acted in accordance with them. That's intentional living.

Did Joseph just stop having emotions? Of course not. He wept when he saw his brothers. Surely, they were bittersweet tears. But he wasn't hijacked by his emotions. He

> **The most effective thing you can do to successfully manage your emotions is to choose to think and behave like Christ.**

controlled his thinking, and that dictated his behavior. Likewise, you'll never stop feeling emotions. Emotional responses will likely start with the first phone call you get today, or the first email, or the first encounter with someone. But you can choose how you'll respond to those emotions.

Do the next right one thing today when you face an emotional trigger that can lead to a hijacked emotion. Here are five to choose from:

1. Be mindful of how you're feeling at that moment, but don't act on it.
2. Tell yourself the truth. "I'm in charge of my emotions. They aren't in charge of me."
3. Ask, "What's the right way to respond to how I'm feeling?"
4. Consider, "How will I feel tomorrow if I react negatively to what I'm feeling right now?"
5. Be swift to listen and slow to speak. Think twice and speak once.

Bold Move Questions: DECLARE who's in charge of your emotions.

1. What do others do that tends to light up my emotional fuse?

   _____

   _____

2. How do I generally respond to that fuse being lit?

   _____

   _____

3. What next right one thing could I do to change how I respond to be more positive and in charge of my emotions?

   _____

   _____

Bold Move Questions: DECLUTTER your emotions.

1. What emotions do I feel when I think about my childhood memories?

   _____

   _____

2. Do I still struggle with those same emotions?

   _____

   _____

3. What did I learn from my siblings when I asked if they have the same childhood memories as me? In what ways are their childhood memories different than mine?

___

Bold Move Questions: DO the next right one thing.

1. How do I struggle with compulsive behaviors?

___

2. What are the emotional roots of those behaviors?

___

3. What can I do differently to address those behaviors so that I am in charge of them?

___

2

The Emotional Languages of Head, Heart, and Hand

Emotions have a profound impact. As host of my radio program and podcast, I hear the toll hijacked emotions have taken in the voices of those who call in to the program. One of those callers, Linda from Wyoming, shared how she struggled with anger that was so volatile, it was damaging to her and those she cared about.

"Has this explosive anger been a life pattern for you?" I asked.

"Interestingly enough," she replied, "it was one of the first things that the Lord dealt with when I became a Christian, and then it tapered off and wasn't an issue. I married into an abusive relationship and came out of it. Now that I'm in another relationship, my anger is resurfacing in a very nasty way."

Emotions such as anger are often symptoms of something deeper within you. I like to refer to it as emotional ooze. It's like a volcano. It may appear dormant, but the magma within continues to build until it starts seeping out as lava in advance of the inevitable eruption. Emotions that are stuffed down will eventually explode into regrettable eruptions of words or actions if not intentionally managed. Some signs of emotional ooze are passive/aggressiveness, sarcasm, moodiness, avoidance, procrastination, withholding affection, and even a change in your expression. Eyes are the window to the soul and can portray emotions such as sadness, loneliness, and anger.

Like Linda, you may wrestle with one negative emotion that tends to hijack your life and steal your happiness and well-being. There are many negative emotions to pick from: anxiety, fear, guilt, envy, shyness, jealousy, and loneliness are just a few. Yet you can take charge of those emotions and redirect that powerful emotional energy from negativity into spiritual, personal, and relational growth. You can harness your God-given emotions and use them to help you boldly live an intentional life in Christ.

Emotions such as anger are often symptoms of something deeper within you.

Proverbs 28:1 says, "The wicked flee though no one pursues, but the righteous are as bold as a lion." Boldness is courage in the face of fear. In fact, I believe boldness is courage in the face of *any* negative emotion ready to hijack your life and run you into an emotional ditch. In order to manage your emotions, you have to be willing to confront some of the deep-rooted issues of your life and find balance so that you can live the way you were created to live. Usually, there are warning signs that are overlooked or neglected that quietly point out the risk of a potential hijacking.

My son, Derek, was still in high school when he came home one afternoon and parked his car in the driveway behind mine. I needed to move his car, so I got in and turned on the ignition. I immediately noticed a warning light blinking on his dashboard. This one indicated that a headlight or taillight was out.

After moving the car, I went inside and approached my son. "Derek, how long have you had a warning light on in your car?"

He shrugged. "Oh, maybe four months. I don't know."

I shook my head in fatherly frustration. "Those lights connect to something, you know. There's probably something going on. Could we check it out?" We did, and sure enough, it was a taillight, and he got it fixed.

In the same way, there are warning lights that flash on the dashboard of your heart before an emotional hijacking takes place. In the beginning, they're easy to ignore. Like Derek's taillight, it doesn't seem that big of a deal. But after your emotion is hijacked, you often look back and realize you saw the warning light. You just didn't do anything about it. Then there are those times the warning light is more urgent. If your car is beginning to overheat, you see the needle going up on the temperature gauge and understand that if you ignore it, you're going to stall or worse.

Freedom from Hijacked Emotions

Make a Bold Move: DECIDE who's in charge of your emotions.

1. Don't ignore emotional warning signs in your life. Taking care of a hijacked emotion early will save you additional pain later on.
2. Freedom starts by discovering the source of your hijacked emotions and intentionally deciding who's in charge.
3. Don't blame others for your emotions—own them!
4. Take action starting today to address your emotional warning signs.

The way to best heed the warning lights in your emotional life is to cultivate a balance of head (healthy thinking), heart (healthy emotions), and hands (healthy behaviors). The healthiest people I know think clearly, feel deeply, and act decisively. The challenge is to discover which of the three—head, heart, or hand— is out of balance with the others. Many of the emotional conflicts we face are the result of our thinking, emotions, and behaviors being out of alignment. Imagine the kind of emotional hijacking that often takes place when a "head person" is married to a "heart person," or when a "hand person" works with a "head person?" The head person wants to think about it, the heart person wants to experience it, and the hand person wants to get it done. Many of our emotional and relational challenges originate from these three. In most situations, we tend to gravitate to our primary language. Keep in mind that there is no one person whose language is all

The Emotional Languages of Head, Heart, and Hand

head, or all heart, or all hand. Emotionally mature people learn to speak the necessary language at the moment when it is needed the most. For example, I primarily identify as a head person, but I've learned to speak the languages of my heart and hand as well. So, while we are never perfectly one or the other, whichever language represents our primary language is where hijacked emotions may start.

THE LANGUAGE OF THE HEAD PERSON

The head person tends to be analytical, factual, and more responsive to details—a "bottom line" sort of person. As a head person, I love to get to the bottom line first, and then I'll push for the details to make sure the bottom line adds up. I've learned that others need to walk step-by-step through the entire process before getting to the bottom line.

Sometimes a head person can feel frustrated because they are often locked in their own minds analyzing, processing, and deciding something to the point that they fail to express what they're thinking. When they finally do say something, they tend to connect with people through ideas versus feelings. One of the signs you're dealing with a head person is when you ask them how they feel, and they tell you what they think. When I'm counseling a head person and get a cognitive response instead of an emotional one, I'll say, "No. Tell me how you *feel*." They'll simply respond, "I just did!"

When arguing with a head person, don't say phrases like "you never" or "you always" because they'll immediately recall that one time when that wasn't true about them.

Freedom from Hijacked Emotions

The head person thrives on facts and details, and they are more likely to challenge whatever you say that doesn't feel logical. Therefore, the head person can win disputes, but they can lose relationships because they miss discerning the heart of the other person. The heart person wants to hear they are loved while the head person is thinking, "I told you 'I love you' when we married, and if I ever change my mind, I'll let you know."

Head people often struggle with experiencing and expressing their emotions—unless it's anger. Many times, their emotions will bottle up inside, like magma within a volcano, and when it's released, there's an explosion. If you're a heart or hand person, you can see why a head person can frustrate you and cause your own emotions to get hijacked. Hopefully, though, you can also realize how they can become frustrated with someone who doesn't understand the language of the head person.

In addition, head people can often unknowingly be insensitive to the needs of others because everything starts in their head. I came home one day and drove into the garage—only to notice a scratch all the way from the front to the back of my wife's car. It wasn't a dent. It could be easily fixed. I knew it wasn't major and assumed Donna was okay, but she had been in some sort of an accident. As I looked at the car, my first thought, being the head person I am, was, *Huh. Wonder what she did?* I walked into the house and saw her sitting at the table.

"What did you do to the car?" I asked inquisitively.

I saw it instantly in her eyes. My question had hurt her, and her response was understandably curt. "I'm fine, thanks."

The Emotional Languages of Head, Heart, and Hand

I could see that Donna was fine. I had processed that she was fine. I *knew* she was fine. If there had been blood on the floor, I would've known differently. It wasn't that I didn't care about her—but I certainly failed to connect with her heart. She wanted to hear me say, "What happened? Are you okay?" I needed to find a better way to communicate, connect my head language with her heart, and express that *she* was what really mattered most to me, not the car.

Later, Donna shared what had caused the supposedly insignificant scratch: an approaching driver had turned into the lane to her left in such a way that had he been one inch closer, he would've hit her head-on. Unbeknownst to me, Donna was still struggling with the fact that she could've been seriously injured or worse when I asked her my seemingly innocuous question. There I was, a head person who allegedly wants the facts, and I didn't even bother to get the facts first. Had I done so, I would've had a better chance to show Donna I cared.

> **Head people often struggle with experiencing and expressing their emotions.**

Make a Bold Move: DECLUTTER your emotions.

1. If you're a head person, be aware that you can easily hurt the feelings of a heart person, miss the priority concerns of a hand person, and painfully "butt heads" with either one.
2. Head people often stuff their emotions. God has given us the gift of emotion, so become

mindful of each experience identifying what you're feeling at that moment. It may be a stretch—but it's worth it.
3. Head people need to guard against over analyzing things to the point of missing what others are feeling and trying to communicate. When talking with someone, take time to make eye contact and listen for the meaning beyond the words.

If you live with a head person, I encourage you to find out what interests them. If your son, for example, wants everything to have a bottom line, your best approach is to come at him with facts. Put things in terms he'll understand. To other head people, I exhort you to be present with people more than with facts. Listen without giving an immediate answer. Ask them how they're feeling without telling them what to do.

THE LANGUAGE OF THE HEART PERSON

Heart people are more aware of the emotional experiences going on with people around them than head or hand people. When we leave an event with a group of people, Donna can easily recall things about them and their relationships that I totally missed while busily doing what head people do best: counting the numbers of chairs, assessing the square footage of the room, and working out how much better I would've organized things had I been in charge.

Heart people are emotional, intuitive, reactive, and passionate. For them, most things begin in the heart. They feel and show intimacy through words and emotions. Heart people often react more quickly to situations, can appear to the head or hand person to be responding illogically, and can be easily hurt or offended by the head or hand person when they never had any intention to do so.

I regularly talk to couples where a head person husband is married to a heart person wife. They experience frustration in their relationship because he often thinks she is too emotional or irrational, while she feels he just doesn't understand what they are going through. "If you loved me," she says, "you'd listen." Yet he fears that if he opens up and starts to talk, there will be no end to the discussion. Both believe their spouse is unaware of their hurt, and sometimes feel that their spouse doesn't care at all. This is why it's so important to learn one another's language.

Make a Bold Move: DECLUTTER your emotions.

1. As a heart person, your gift of emotional awareness can also become your greatest enemy. Identify right now the one emotion that hijacks your life the most.
2. As a heart person, take the emotion you just identified and start a 30-day challenge to daily take control of that one emotion.
3. One step to declutter your emotions is to decide today to use your emotions—and not be used by them.

Freedom from Hijacked Emotions

My daughter, Andrea, is a heart person. When she was a teenager, her big-hearted approach to life and others caused her dad's head to go into overdrive trying to help her think everything through. Not long after graduating from college, Andrea came home to visit and shared with me and Donna what God was doing in her life. As we sat in the living room, she revealed, "I feel God is calling me to the mission field."

> **Heart people are emotional, intuitive, reactive, and passionate.**

The idea wasn't anything new. She had been on mission trips to Mexico in high school, and we knew her heart could be drawn to overseas mission work. Still, we weren't prepared for her declaration. Sensing Donna's concern, I asked the obvious. "Where do you think He's calling you to go?"

"Well," she said. "I asked the missions agency, 'Where in the world is the place that nobody else is willing to go?' They said, 'We have openings right now for 100 missionaries in Mongolia, and we only have 14 people who are willing to go.' So, I told them, 'I'll go.'"

Mongolia? I don't even know where that is? I started running through a checklist of head person worries. What are the dangers there? What is the culture like? Where will she live? What is the bottom line for what she is trying to do? She told us she was interested in teaching English and sharing Christ with the people and assured us she would be safe.

After several months of extensive training, our precious and only daughter packed her bags, got on a plane all by herself, and flew to the most remote part of Outer Mongolia, a land in Asia sandwiched between Russia and China. Andrea went there, and to the people living in this remote place, because she cares for others, and it was where she felt the Lord wanted her to be. Since then, Andrea has married a wonderful Christian man named Kris who is a helicopter pilot. Along with her husband and three of our grandchildren, she now serves in one of the poorest and most dangerous countries in West Africa. They live with bars on the windows of their house and a 24-hour-a-day guard at the door—but Donna and I, while still concerned about her in our own ways as head and heart people, couldn't be prouder of Andrea and her family.

THE LANGUAGE OF THE HAND PERSON

The hand person loves lists and getting things done. To them, acts of service mean everything. They want to take action and see results. For that very reason, hand people can appear to be very impatient. They can also be intolerant of words that are not backed up by action, or they can become so busy with their activity that they miss what's going on around them. They have to guard against projects replacing people in importance.

Trustworthiness is huge with the hand person. You might casually say to them, "I'll take out the trash later," but then you forget and it doesn't get thrown out. By morning, you've hurt their feelings. They have experienced a breach of trust. Head and heart people also expect trustworthiness in relationships, but for the hand person, hijacked emotions can be heightened due to their priority language of "getting things done." They often measure how much someone cares by how many things get checked off their "to do" list. You may think it's no big deal, but all they know is that you told them you were going to do something and then you didn't follow through. A hand person looks at someone's behavior and uses those factors to determine how close they are going to get to that person. When you interact with a hand person, especially those you love, you must show love in terms of action. Do the dishes without being asked and see what happens. Doing things for them communicates that you value them.

> **The hand person loves lists and getting things done.**

My wife, Donna, is also a hand person. I've learned there are two things that mean a great deal to her. If I clean up my messes and fill up the gas tank in her car, I clearly show affection to her. It's like I'm filling up her love tank, too. When Donna accompanies me to a conference, she wants to stay busy helping out at the resource table. Just sitting still drives her crazy. She wants to be out there helping our team and serving attendees. She has no desire to be on the platform. Rather, Donna loves to stay busy at home, works from a checklist, and is typically always looking for the next project.

The other day I came home from work to observe a new paint sample on the wall. It was an interesting tinge of green.

"What do you think of that?" Donna asked.

"I don't like it," I replied politely but honestly.

When I came in the next day, the sample was gone.

Where did it go? I thought. Donna then held up a paint can. "Will you put this in the garage?"

I took it and saw it was a can of the green I had rejected the day before. As I stepped into the garage, I noticed, not for the first time, how many other cans of paint were beginning to accumulate. I found a marker nearby and I wrote on the top of one of the cans in front, "Another good idea."

The next day, Donna brought that very can to me.

"Another good idea, huh?" she asked, smiling.

We laughed. We knew it was my way of showing my appreciation of her desire to take care of our home as a hand person, and of acknowledging our differences as individuals.

Make a Bold Move: DEVELOP a plan of action to respond to emotional triggers.

1. As a hand person, guard against taking on too many things. Overcommitment may make you feel needed and busy, but it can wear you out spiritually, physically, and emotionally.
2. Intentionally establish more margin in your schedule.
3. Identify the next right one thing you could drop off your daily checklist, starting today.

OUR DIFFERENCES COMPLEMENT ONE ANOTHER

God made us different so that we'd need each other. As Proverbs 27:17 declares, "As iron sharpens iron, so one person sharpens another." If you're a head person, you need a heart person in your life to help you stay in touch with what's going on in your world. If you're a heart person, you need a head person in your life to keep your feet on the ground. Every single one of us needs a hand person in our lives to help us accomplish those things that need to be done. It's exactly as 1 Corinthians 12 declares about the body of Christ, the family of Christian believers. "Just as a body, though one, has many parts, but all its many parts form one body, so it is with Christ ... The eye cannot say to the hand, 'I don't need you!' And the head cannot say to the feet, 'I don't need you!' On the contrary, those parts of the body that seem to be weaker are indispensable, and the parts that we think are less honorable we treat with special honor." (1 Corinthians 12:12, 21-23)

Remember, intentionality can only occur when you combine information, insight, *and* action. You could put it like this: **Information + Insight + Action = An Intentional Life.** Information comes from the head, insight from the heart, and action from the hand. All three are vital.

Good intentions only become reality when you are diligent to take action. A good intention without action is only a good idea. You can have all the passion for a vision, but unless you take action, nothing happens. Ephesians 5:10 tells you to "figure out what will please Christ, and then do it." (TM) If you really look at that directive closely, you can see how the head, heart, and hand are each necessary to fulfill it. To *figure out* means to think it through. That is using your head. You discover *what will*

The Emotional Languages of Head, Heart, and Hand

please Christ by connecting your heart to Him. You *then do it* by putting your hands to the task.

My oldest son, Evan, is a hand and head person. He thrives on getting things done with excellence and to God's glory. When he succeeded me as President of Family Life Communications, the Board of Directors knew the ministry would be in good hands, literally, into the next generation. I've observed how Evan has intentionally expanded his range of leadership gifts to include a huge heart for the staff and listeners as well. Evan's leadership growth reminds us that when we were created, God, in His intentional design, created us as head, heart, and hand people. There was perfect balance. Adam and Eve had perfect communication, perfect understanding, and perfect ability in getting things done. When sin occurred, things got shattered and we gravitated to one of these three. Whenever our primary language goes into overdrive, hijacked emotions become a threat to a balanced life. Yet it's in reestablishing that balance between head, heart, and hand in our relationships that will deliver the results we desire in the five essential areas of life: faith, relationships, health, finances, and work.

Bold Move Questions: DECIDE who's in charge of your emotions.

1. What are three emotional warning signs in my life right now?

_____

_____

2. Where do I think they are coming from?

_____

_____

3. Who do I blame for these emotions?

_____

_____

4. What's the next right one thing I can do this month to address these warning signs?

_____

_____

Bold Move Questions: DECLUTTER your emotions.

1. As a head person, how has overthinking or overanalyzing gotten me in trouble with a heart or hand person?

_____

_____

The Emotional Languages of Head, Heart, and Hand

2. In what ways is it difficult for me to name and identify my emotions?

3. What next right one thing could I do over the next 30 days to stop overanalyzing things to the point I miss what others are feeling and trying to communicate to me?

Bold Move Questions: DECLUTTER your emotions.

1. What emotion gives me the biggest challenge as a heart person? Why?

2. What are the strengths of a heart person?

3. As a heart person, what next right one thing could I do in the next 30 days that will help me deal with a negative emotion?

Freedom from Hijacked Emotions

Bold Move Questions: DEVELOP a plan of action to respond to emotional triggers.

1. As a hand person, how does taking on too much negatively impact my life?

___

___

2. What can I do to establish more margin in my schedule?

___

___

3. What is the next right one thing I could drop from my "to do" list to add that margin to my life?

___

___

3

Tell Yourself the Truth

It's impossible to shut off self-talk. Our internal dialogue is up and running all day long and will continue until the day we stop breathing. Even when we sleep, buried thoughts emerge in our dreams. Millions of dollars are spent weekly on meditation and yoga-type programs designed to help people control their thoughts and quiet their minds. The Bible speaks directly to self-talk when it exhorts us to "take captive every thought to make it obedient to Christ" (2 Corinthians 10:5) because a double-minded person is "unstable in all they do." (James 1:8).

How do you deal with your self-talk? Is it your enemy or your friend? Self-talk will either lift you up or bring you down. Even more, it'll either improve your relationships or damage them. It's common for us to repeat self-lies or half-truths about ourselves without even being aware of how those lies adversely impact our decision making and undermine our emotional well-being. I do my best to never make an important decision when I know my thinking and emotions have been hijacked in some way. For me, worrying about making the perfect decision can place me into a mental and emotional cul-de-sac, going around in circles without making any progress.

SELF LIES ARE STILL LIES

We teach our children early on that lying is a sin, so is lying to ourselves any less of a transgression? I don't think so; a lie is still a lie even if it's about you from you. In fact, negative self-talk is even more devious because those untruths can become foundational to how you see yourself, usurping reality.

> **We teach our children early on that lying is a sin, so is lying to ourselves any less of a transgression?**

Many years ago, I was in a serious car accident. It took place just north of Jackson, Michigan at the corner of M-50 and Rives Junction Road. I was coming home from the Family Life Radio studio when I pulled up to the intersection. It's a high-traffic area with cars traveling up to 60 miles per hour at the crossing. Opposite from me, the car heading in my direction was waiting at the stop sign for the traffic to clear so the driver could proceed. Suddenly, the vehicle pulled out right in front of another car travelling at top speed. Everything went into slow motion as the cars collided, causing both to roll over—and right onto my vehicle. All three cars were totaled, and though my car was propelled backward about 20 feet, crushing the hood and engine, my seat belt was fastened, and I escaped with only a few bruises. I didn't even have to go to the hospital.

That accident happened way back in 1981, yet when I return to Michigan each year and drive up to the intersection of M-50 and Rives Junction Road, something starts to happen inside of me. My heart starts to pound, and I feel my blood pressure soar. It seems so illogical. Why would I react that way so many years after the event? Maybe it was because the other drivers involved in the accident never saw it coming, but I did, long enough to know, *I see where this is going, and it's not going to be good.* If someone were to ask me, "What is the most dangerous intersection in America?" I would tell them M-50 and Rives Junction Road. Is that the truth? Of course not. In fact, it may be one of the safest intersections in the country, but you'd have a hard time convincing me. It's an untruth that became truth to me because of my experience. Self-lies aren't logical, and often, our emotions aren't either.

The list of the possible untruths you can believe is long, and each one can detrimentally impact your decisions and emotions:

1. **Nothing will ever change.** This untruth robs you of allowing God His rightful place in your life. It replaces His limitless view of your life and intentional plans for your future with your own limited, undersized negativity. Don't restrict God's big aspirations for your life with your distorted view of "what could be," for God declares, "I know

the plans I have for you … plans to prosper you and not to harm you, plans to give you hope and a future." (Jeremiah 29:11)

2. **This is just who I am.** This untruth prevents you from experiencing God's aim to lead you along the path of growth and maturity. Don't settle. If your self-talk today is the same as it was three years ago, it's time to get intentional with your life.

3. **I have the right to feel this way.** If you've been hurt, you may believe that hanging on to your pain is your right. Doing so gives you a sense of security and control. But do you benefit from hanging on to those emotions? Letting go can be difficult and scary, but if you don't, those negative emotions will become a weight around your neck that steals away God's purposes for your life. In 1 Corinthians 10:23, Paul provided this perspective: "'I have the right to do anything,' you say—but not everything is beneficial. 'I have the right to do anything'—but not everything is constructive."

4. **I shouldn't feel this way.** The opposite of hanging on to negative emotions is denying they exist or feeling guilty whenever they surface. Both will keep you from experiencing your emotions so that you can use them to make a change. Paul tells you to put off falsehood and speak truthfully before addressing the emotion of anger, saying, "'In your anger do not sin': Do not let the sun go down while you are still angry." (Ephesians 4:26) You have the power through God to control your emotions and not allow them to be hijacked.

5. **It's my fault.** This can be true, and when it is, the healthy response is to own up to it and take responsibility. But taking on fault when it's not truly yours can be a form of pride. It will make you needlessly feel responsible for things beyond your control, and that can be damaging to your spirit.
6. **If God loved me, this wouldn't be happening to me.** An extension of believing something is your fault is wrongly passing blame onto God, but this untruth will rob you of your intimacy with Him. We live in a broken world. Bad things do happen to good people. Yet it's easy for us to feel that life isn't fair, but act like it's supposed to be. That's no way to think or live. Ecclesiastes 9:2 teaches you that "all share a common destiny—the righteous and the wicked, the good and the bad, the clean and the unclean, those who offer sacrifices and those who do not. As it is with the good, so with the sinful; as it is with those who take oaths, so with those who are afraid to take them." That's an outlook based on truth. You can overcome your "life isn't fair" self-talk lie by focusing on your strengths, gifts, and blessings from God, remaining mindful that God's path is different for each person, and rejoicing when others succeed.

> **Self-lies aren't logical, and often, our emotions aren't either.**

7. **My opinions don't matter.** This self-talk lie will

cheat you from developing and sharing your insights and creativity with others. It's a small step from "my opinions don't count" to "I must not be capable of doing great things." Remember, God used very ordinary people to change the world. David was a shepherd. Peter was a fisherman. Lydia sold cloth. God seldom used the biggest, strongest, or wisest. In fact, He "chose the weak things of the world to shame the strong." (1 Corinthians 1:27)

8. **I'm such an idiot.** It's one thing to say this to yourself when you accidentally lock your keys in the car or spill a cup of coffee. It's quite another thing to apply it broadly to who you believe you are. You are a child of God, and your Heavenly Father created you with incredible value and self-worth. That's the truth. Instead, turn your self-talk around to comply with Philippians 4:8, my life verse, where Paul instructs, "Whatever is true, whatever is noble, whatever is right, whatever is pure, whatever is lovely, whatever is admirable—if anything is excellent or praiseworthy—think about such things." What is noble about yourself? Admirable? Praiseworthy?

9. **Other people have it all together.** This lie undermines who you are in Christ. In I Corinthians 12, Paul reminds you that it takes each part of the body to make a unified whole. Others may appear to

> **It's easy for us to feel that life isn't fair, but act like it's supposed to be.**

have it all together, but in reality, they may be only showing what they want others to see. We need one another. Each one of us is vital. That's God's design.
10. **It's too late.** No, it's not. Don't allow this lie to rob you of your future. God's love, grace, and ability to forgive and restore is endless, and He can do "immeasurably more than all we ask or imagine, according to his power that is at work within us." (Ephesians 3:20)

Make a Bold Move: DEVELOP a plan of action to respond to emotional triggers.

1. Telling yourself lies makes for a mediocre life. Identify any of the untruths from the list of 10 above that you struggle with and develop a plan of action to confront them.
2. Part of your action plan should include telling any untruth to leave and that they're not welcome back into your life.
3. Live in truth today to become the way God intends for you to become tomorrow. You can do this!

BACK TO THE BEGINNING

In Arizona, many people don't have grassy lawns. We have decorative rocks in our yards. One day, after I had 20 tons of rock delivered to my home via a couple of big trucks, I decided I could move and arrange the stones myself. So, being a head person, (which, in my case, is a nice way of saying "being stubborn"), I sat down with my spreadsheet and laid out in advance how long it was going to take me to move 20 tons of rock. My wife, a hand person, drew on her knowledge and past experiences of watching me trying to do everything myself, and told me, "You shouldn't be doing that. You'll have a heart attack!"

"Yes, I can," I responded, then repeated to myself, *Yes, you can. All you have to do is plan it out.* And I did. My spreadsheet said I could do it all in three days.

At the end of the second day, I had moved about five tons. Impressive, perhaps, but I still had 15 tons to go! The next day, we had pizza delivered, and when the delivery boy, a wispy 18-year-old kid, handed me the pizza, I spied his name badge. "Hey, Chad. You want some extra hours?"

Okay, so I hired the pizza kid to help me move the rest of the rocks.

My prideful self-talk about the rocks was a lie, and I was so painfully feeling the effects that I had to get some help. Instead of telling myself the truth (and listening to my wife) from the very beginning, I struggled through unnecessary fatigue and soreness. Lesson learned.

I didn't do what I should've done from the start because my thinking was out of whack. The Apostle Paul understood this well. He said, "I do not understand what I do. For what I want to do I do not do, but what I hate I do … I have the desire to do what is good, but I cannot carry it out. For I do not do the good I want to do, but the evil I do not want to do—this I keep on doing. Now if I do what I do not want to do, it is no longer I who do it, but it is sin living in me that does it." (Romans 7:15,

18-20) Paul was no different than the rest of us. We can all become captive to wrong thinking about our emotions that lead to wrong responses to them.

Where does the tendency to listen to self-talk lies come from? It goes all the way back to the beginning. In the Bible, Genesis starts telling the great story of God's intentional love for us. In Chapters 1 and 2, we discover how the Lord created Adam and Eve. It's a beautiful account until we reach Chapter 3 where disaster strikes in the form of sin. The rest of Scripture delivers the miraculous conclusion of the story, filled with tragedy and miracles.

Adam and Eve were the first man and woman to have a perfect relationship with God. Their thinking, emotions, and behaviors were untainted and pure. They knew nothing of lies or untruthful self-talk—until a fateful conversation took place involving Satan, disguised as a serpent, and Eve. "Now the serpent was more crafty than any of the wild animals the Lord God had made. He said to the woman, 'Did God really say, "You must not eat from any tree in the garden?"' The woman said to the serpent, 'We may eat fruit from the trees in the garden, but God did say, "You must not eat fruit from the tree that is in the middle of the garden, and you must not touch it, or you will die."' (Genesis 3:1-3)

Eve spoke the truth to Satan, repeating to him what God had told her and Adam. But look how Satan responds:

"'You will not certainly die,' the serpent said to the woman. 'For God knows that when you eat from it your eyes will be opened, and you will be like God, knowing good and evil.'" (Genesis 3:4-5)

He lied—and that lie led Eve into deceitful self-talk. "When the woman saw that the fruit of the tree was good for food and pleasing to the eye, and also desirable for gaining wisdom, she took some and ate it. She also gave some to her husband, who was with her, and he ate it. Then the eyes of both of them were opened, and they realized they were naked; so they sewed fig leaves together and made coverings for themselves." (Genesis 3:6-7)

Do you see what happened? The moment Adam and Eve ate, they were emotionally hijacked. Suddenly, they "realized they were naked" and felt that was wrong. It hadn't been before, but it was now. They became captive to wrong thinking about their emotions that led to a wrong response. The cycle that affects each one of us all these eons later was activated.

THE START OF SHAME

Something else began that terrible day. Shame entered into the lives of humanity. That's what Adam and Eve experienced when they felt the need to cover themselves. In Genesis 2:25 we are told, "Adam and his wife were both naked, and they felt no shame." Yet when sin occurred, shame showed up. Merriam-Webster defines shame as "a painful emotion caused by consciousness of guilt, shortcoming, or impropriety." It's that excruciating sense of having done something wrong or knowing that things just aren't right. Adam and Eve went from self-deception to shame, and then that shame caused them to be uncomfortably conscious about themselves.

An uncomfortable sense of self can cause us to do and believe stupid things. We refuse to be real with other people. We become self-protective and hide out from other people. We struggle to be who we are in our relationships because of shame. There's always a sense we won't measure up.

When you look in the mirror, do you see the creation of God looking back at you, or do you feel uncomfortable about yourself? You should see the creation of God, but if you're honest, that's likely not what you see most of the time. Instead, we see all of the things we don't like about ourselves. Jean Baudrillard, a French theorist, once described "one of life's primal situations; the game of hide and seek. Oh, the delicious thrill of hiding while the others come looking for you, the delicious terror of being discovered, but what panic when, after a long search, the others abandon you! You mustn't hide too well. You mustn't be too good at the game. The player must never be bigger than the game itself."[1] We can play hide and seek in our relationships and with God as a result of shame.

Another reason Adam and Eve covered themselves is because they didn't want to be exposed. On that day in Genesis, spiritual heart damage occurred in their lives—and we struggle every day with the same affliction. We usually can't make it through an entire day without our emotions being ravaged as a result of shame and the deceptive self-talk it creates.

SELF-DECEPTION ALSO MAKES US BLIND

I was talking on my radio program and podcast one afternoon about the sanctity of marriage when Sarah called from Alaska. "I'm a Christian," she declared. "I'm a follower of Christ. But I'm single and living with a man."

It was instantly clear that she saw nothing wrong with that, so I challenged her.

"Well, tell me a little bit about your spirit. How does this affect your spirit?"

She replied, "Well, Randy, it's better than me going from man to man to man."

Sarah had convinced herself that it was okay to live with a man even though she wasn't married to him. As we continued our conversation, she further revealed that he was married to another woman. In her self-deception, she concluded that having an adulterous relationship with one man was better than sleeping with different men every night. In her mind, it made total sense.

Satan is a deceiver who "leads the whole world astray." (Revelation 12:9) The author of deception, "when he lies, he speaks his native language, for he is a liar and the father of lies." (John 8:44) Yet the decision to doubt God and His truth is *ours,* and when we deceive ourselves, we can come to the wrong conclusions about our lives in any of the five essential areas: faith, relationships, health, finances, and work.

Make a Bold Move: DO the next right one thing.

1. Focus on telling yourself the next right one thing each day that is true about God in order to build your faith and challenge hijacked emotions.
2. If you're married, start telling yourself the next right one thing daily that is positive and true about your spouse in order to strengthen your marriage. If you're not married, think about your siblings, children, co-workers, or friends.
3. Focus on doing one new thing each day to improve your health, and it will change your life.
4. Focus on doing one new positive thing with your money to find financial freedom. Our *Intentional Living* model for financial freedom is to give 10 percent, save 10 percent, and live on the remaining 80 percent.
5. Start the next right one thing (and stop one thing) to thrive at work.

If you are going to live an intentional life in Christ, you have to build your life each day on 100 percent truth, realizing that anything less can become self-deception that convinces us we will feel better if we give in to it. We see how others are deceived and shake our heads, thinking that will never happen to us. But the fact is we judge others differently than we judge ourselves.

For instance, after a long and difficult day at the office one evening, I told myself, *I worked hard today. I really deserve to stop and get some ice cream on the way home.* When that wasn't quite enough to get me to pull over, I added, *And all those people who call me on the radio? I feel so badly for some of them. I think I'll have some ice cream. That'll make me feel better.* So, blindly ignoring the fact I had just made my listeners responsible for my actions, I turned into the parking lot of the ice cream shop. I could actually taste the cool, creamy treat in my mouth as I drove up to the drive-thru to make my order. *Oh, it's really going to be good.*

> **Choose today to embrace God's truth about yourself, your thinking, and your emotions, and your right responses will liberate you.**

Then, as I was licking up the last remnants of my cone, the words of my doctor came to mind, warning me against fat and sugar. The ice cream that I thought would soothe my rough day ended up making me feel guilty about my poor health decision.

EXPECTATIONS−REALITY = DISAPPOINTMENT

When Kim called my program, she got right to the point. "I just get so frustrated, Randy. I really strive to be intentional, to be truthful and proactive in my life, but the people around me—it seems like they're not very intentional at all. I talk to them over and over again about the same things and sometimes I get snappy with them. I don't like them, and I think that's not being very Christian."

I shared with her my relationship formula of how expectations minus reality equals disappointment. "We have a level of expectations that are not being met," I said. "You and I have to ask ourselves if our expectations are reasonable. And frankly, is it my business to expect that from them? Changing your expectations will change your reality."

Kim sighed. "It's hard when you're kind of a perfectionist."

"It is," I agreed. "But this is an inside job. This is not about other people. It's about you."

Placing her high expectations on those around her wasn't going to make her, or them, feel any better. The self-deception was only going to hijack her emotions and cause them to experience the same, perpetuating cycle. I encouraged Kim to start behaving less frustrated by changing her expectations, and to also tell herself the truth by changing her thinking.

Make a Bold Move: DEVELOP a plan of action to respond to emotional triggers.

1. When expectations align with reality, hijacked emotions are seldom a problem. As you practice adjusting your expectations to reality, your emotions will follow.
2. The greater the distance between your

expectations and reality, the greater the potential for your emotions to get hijacked.
3. Today's the day to take control of your emotions. Develop a plan and take the first step.

Remember, self-talk will either lift you up or bring you down. Even more, it'll either improve your relationships or damage them. Choose today to embrace God's truth about yourself, your thinking, and your emotions, and your right responses will liberate you—for "if the Son sets you free, you will be free indeed." (John 8:36)

Bold Move Questions: DEVELOP a plan of action to respond to emotional triggers.

1. What is a damaging lie I tell myself?

   _____

   _____

2. What is a healthy emotional response to situations that aren't fair?

   _____

   _____

3. What is a better thing to tell myself than, "Things will never change?"

   _____

   _____

Bold Move Questions: DO the next right one thing.

1. How have I deceived myself regarding my faith?

   _____

   _____

2. How have I deceived myself regarding my relationships?

   _____

   _____

3. How have I deceived myself regarding my health?

_____

_____

4. How have I deceived myself regarding my finances?

_____

_____

5. How have I deceived myself regarding my work?

_____

_____

Bold Move Questions: DEVELOP a plan of action to respond to emotional triggers.

1. Where have my expectations not aligned with my reality?

_____

_____

2. How has the resulting disappointment impacted my emotional life?

_____

_____

Tell Yourself the Truth

3. What can I change to respond in a healthy way from now on?

_____

_____

4

Taming Anger: The Explosive Hijacker

Earlier, we learned that some people will keep their emotions bottled up inside of them, like magma within a volcano, until they're released in an explosion.

One of those emotions is anger—and this emotion has done more to destroy relationships than probably any other. We tend to lump other emotions under the name of "anger" when, in fact, there are important distinctions to recognize. For example, we may assume that being annoyed, frustrated, agitated, enraged, or wrathful all fall under the anger category, but a person who is annoyed is clearly experiencing something much different than someone who is in a rage.

Consider the following examples that can be perceived as anger:

- Joe is annoyed because some nuisance in his life needs to be addressed.
- Shelley is frustrated and likely experiencing a disappointment that needs to be grieved.
- Justin is agitated and probably perturbed by something in his environment that needs to be buffered.
- Marsha is experiencing wrath and is a danger to herself or others.
- Mack is enraged and beyond rational thought.

Jennifer from Alabama, a caller to my radio show and podcast, shared with me that when she gets stressed, her anger comes out toward those around her or her loved ones. "Dr. Randy, a lot of this has happened within the last year because my husband had a stroke and then a heart attack six months later," she revealed. "We're trying to deal with everything."

"Your anger is a symptom that you're legitimately overwhelmed," I responded. "You've got a boatload of challenges." Then I asked, "What can you do to not allow the stress which is a part of your life to become distress? There's a difference between the two. We all have stress. But when it becomes a problem, then it's distress. What next right one thing can you do to put a little margin back in your life?"

"Maybe start taking better care of myself because I feel like right now everything falls on me. I don't have really any other help."

"You've been worried," I told her. "Your husband has been ill. You've taken on all the responsibility. I'm sure you have some legitimate fears and concerns about the future as a result of this."

Taming Anger: The Explosive Hijacker

As we continued to talk, Jennifer recognized that stress triggered by fear was the *root issue* of her emotional hijacking, not the expressions of anger. It's important to know and understand which emotion you are experiencing in relation to your anger because each one requires a different response. How you choose to respond will make a huge difference in the quality of your relationships, your physical and emotional well-being, and in your effectiveness to bring about positive and constructive change.

Anger is an emotional response to an unmet need, expectation, or injustice. Anger is not sin, but a natural, God-given physiological response to any number of other emotions. Our bodies prepare for action. Yet anger is a double-edged sword. It has the potential to help us protect ourselves and others. It can also be a catalyst to fix problems in marriages and families while helping a person get focused on what truly needs to get done to bring about needed change. But its relative value is largely determined by what we decide to do with it. If not properly dealt with, anger can turn *inward*, resulting in depression, self-mutilation, or changes in eating patterns and sexual function, or *outward*, resulting in physical disturbances including outbursts that can harm ourselves and those around us through abuse, manipulation, or unhealthy control of others.

> **Anger is an emotional response to an unmet need, expectation, or injustice.**

Make a Bold Move: DECLUTTER your emotions.
1. As the Apostle Paul commanded, practice being angry without sinning. Use anger as a fuel to motivate you to positive and healthy action.
2. Doing Bold Move #1 isn't easy. Understanding the root of your anger and intentionally dealing with it will be a great help.
3. When you feel anger coming on, tell yourself the truth. "Anger doesn't own me, and I will not allow it to control my life right now."

CONTROLLING YOUR INITIAL RESPONSE

The emotional and physical numbness triggered by a traumatic event typically gives way to feelings of anger that can range from mild agitation to violent rage. The greater the sense of hurt, fear, and frustration, the greater the intensity of our anger. It is important to remember that our initial or "automatic" response to anger may not be the most constructive. We need to watch our words and our actions so that they do not become a damaging expression of our pain. In addition, the once widely held belief that letting one's anger out through a dramatic release of physical energy, like hitting a pillow, screaming, and throwing things has been offset by research showing that this form of catharsis can actually reinforce the expression of hostility and aggression, which may increase the likelihood of a similar and even more intense response in the future.

Therefore, it's better to acknowledge your anger and its source. Go ahead and admit to yourself and to those around you that you are angry. Simply saying it aloud can help decrease the intensity of your feelings. When you fail to acknowledge your anger, you run the risk of holding it in until it overflows or begins to destroy you physically, spiritually, and emotionally. Feelings that are buried alive do not die! Anger will return more strongly and convincingly unless it is intentionally understood and dealt with properly. There are Christian counselors, psychologists, and anger management courses available in many communities to assist you after you commit to finding freedom from the hijacked emotion of anger.

> **Feelings that are buried alive do not die!**

You have the power of God through His Holy Spirit to also help you deal with your anger and its source. Ephesians 4:31 exhorts us to rely on Him to help us "get rid of all bitterness, rage and anger, brawling and slander, along with every form of malice." This starts by identifying the root of your anger issue. Is it coming from bitterness, which results in feelings of intense animosity toward someone? Has it gotten to the level of wrath, where you have a violent anger which you recognize is out of control, as opposed to clamor, which is a loud, continued noise or forceful complaint? Maybe it's malice, which is manifested in a vindictive spirit to pay back a person for a wrong done to you. Perhaps you've had an experience in your marriage, with a sibling, or even a co-worker where that person seemed to be angry all the time, cutting you off, not returning your phone calls, and treating you with disrespect. You knew they were angry, but you didn't understand what their problem was.

Anger can be expressed in subtle but no less destructive ways as well. Passive-aggressive behavior is a common theme seen in marriage counseling. Since we judge ourselves by our intentions and others by our expectations, subtle expressions of anger are easily justified. For these people, the root issue is avoided and their thinking instead is, "I've told him a thousand times what I need and he never listens, so I'm feeling justified to act this way." That's how Heather was after years of feeling ignored in her marriage. Rather than getting to the root issue, she wielded passive-aggressiveness through moodiness, sarcasm, withdrawing sexually, and overspending to let her husband know she wasn't happy. It confused him and made him say angry things back to her, which only compounded the problem. This had gone on for most of their 22-year marriage.

In counseling, Heather admitted to not taking responsibility for her part of the problem and agreed to be more honest about her feelings and avoid the passive-aggressive responses that only made things worse. Together, she and her husband talked, worked, and prayed through their problems and made a few powerful intentional changes in their marriage. Heather connected her heart hurts to her head and discovered how to express what she was feeling to her husband. Because of her actions, he started dealing with some of his own issues.

ANGER FOR GOOD?

When the Bible instructs us to be angry but not sin (Ephesians 4:26), that tells us that there is such a thing as "good" anger. You might recall Christ's response to the money changers in the temple (Matthew 21:12-13). He overturned tables and drove people out of the courts. That's certainly an angry response, but it was good because He was responding to what He saw as an injustice before God and an improper use of the temple itself.

Roots of bitterness, pride, and the need to control can result in anger that is both sinful and self-destructive, but roots of injustice and things that hurt the heart of God can result in the kind of anger that leads to change, if used in an intentional way.

Here's how this looks:

- Roots of bitterness result in getting even
- Roots of envy result in competition
- Roots of pride result in passive-aggressiveness
- Roots of hurt result in moodiness

When the roots of anger grow in the soil of selfishness, the result will be selfish outcomes. However, when the roots grow in the soil of love for others and glorifying God, the results will be other-focused.

- Roots of concern result in intentional actions of kindness
- Roots of love result in intentional actions of caring for others

- Roots of injustice result in intentional actions for justice

As a child, I remember eavesdropping on my parents as they talked in the front seat of our car on the way to church each Sunday. Leaning forward to catch their conversation, I often heard things like, "What would our church do if all of these children were to show up each Sunday?" as we drove by underprivileged children. Even as a boy, I knew our church was likely not equipped to minister effectively to such needy kids.

That angered my parents—in a very *good* way, as it turned out. They saw an injustice, and it drove them to intentionally do something. They didn't yell, protest, or blame the government or the church. They acted, and it changed our lives. In 1968, my father, Morry, decided to leave his career as a businessperson, sell the house and all the unnecessary stuff we had collected over the years, and move our family to a small village in the heart of Michigan. There, together with my mother, Dorothy, they started a ranch for underprivileged boys and girls so they could come to camp, learn about God, and experience His creation. My brother, Larry, and his wife, Cheri, joined my parents to operate the first Youth Haven in Rives Junction, Michigan and later a second ranch in Picacho, Arizona, leading the ministry into a second generation.

Today, a third generation of Carlsons oversee the ministry. Anger, channeled positively, has had a generational effect in my family and has impacted the lives of tens of thousands of children for the better.

Taming Anger: The Explosive Hijacker

Make a Bold Move: DECIDE who's in charge of your emotions.

1. The healthy response to anger over injustice is to do something. Intentionally do the next right one thing to improve the life of another person. Serve. Speak up with confident respect. Positive action will help to control hijacked emotions.
2. Share with someone in need today.
3. Ask God to show you the next right one thing you can do in the face of injustice.
4. Enjoy the feeling of helping others.

WHEN YOU'RE THE ANGRY ONE

If you're someone who struggles with anger, you likely already know its destructive results in your relationships and your life. Perhaps you feel you have no control over this "hot emotion." It seems to bubble up from nowhere, and at times the littlest provocation can set you off. Yet as you recognize the consequences of uncontrolled anger, that should motivate you to take a disciplined and intentional approach to overcome. It is an emotion that you can conquer!

Ephesians 4:32 directs you to "be kind and compassionate to one another, forgiving each other, just as in Christ God forgave you." **Kindness + Love = Forgiveness** is the formula that will take you where you need to go in dealing with your anger and how you respond to it. In addition, here are some constructive self-talk ideas that will help you tell yourself the truth about anger:

- "When I respond to my anger irrationally or aggressively, it will not serve any positive purpose."
- "It is good to express my anger in a healthy, God-honoring fashion."
- "Ultimately, God is in control and His purposes will prevail."

In addition, as you start to see others as individuals with needs, desires, and wants—and work through prayer and practice to focus on meeting those needs, desires, and wants—your levels of frustration and anger toward others will be diffused.

Why is anger a problem for you? Perhaps you grew up in a home where anger was used to control difficult situations. Maybe you learned through repetitive practice that anger worked for your parents or your siblings and found that it worked for you, too. As humans, we tend to fall back onto learned patterns of behavior, either good or bad. Habits have a way of persisting. Charles Duhigg, in his acclaimed book, *The Power of Habit*, writes that habits are "the choices that all of us deliberately make at some point, and then stop thinking about but continue doing."[1] It's the habitual nature of emotional habits that make them both a blessing and a curse. When emotional habits are healthy, you will thrive, but when emotional habits are unhealthy, they result in ill health relationally and sometimes physically.

Anger may also be present in your life because you have areas of unforgiveness. It could be that you've been through a bitter divorce, a loss of employment, serious health issues, or some other loss in your life. Each one tends to have a compounding effect, and unless you properly deal with them, anger is often the result.

Consider for a moment the last three anger episodes in your life:

- Where were you?
- Who was involved?
- What was said?
- What were you thinking and feeling just before you became aware that you were angry?

Don't be surprised if you start to see a pattern. As you begin to identify some of the triggers that initiate your emotions, you will be able to prepare yourself for the next time they come around. For instance, limit your exposure to the things (and, if you are able, the people) that trigger your anger. If you find, for example, that your anger intensifies when you watch the news on TV or online, then you may need to significantly reduce the time you expose yourself to these negative images. Find positive and constructive alternative activities such as exercising, reading a book, playing with your children, community volunteer work, or even watching a funny movie. Give yourself a break to help you keep your perspective.

> **It's the habitual nature of emotional habits that make them both a blessing and a curse.**

FORGIVING THE OFFENDERS

As we deal with our anger, we must come to the place where we are willing to model Christ's example of forgiveness, expressed so poignantly toward His torturers when He was on the cross at His greatest point of suffering. Jesus said, "Father, forgive them, for they do not know what they are doing." (Luke 23:34)

God expects us to forgive. At the close of His model prayer in Matthew 6, Jesus said, "If you forgive other people when they sin against you, your heavenly Father will also forgive you. But if you do not forgive others their sins, your Father will not forgive your sins." (Matthew 6:14-15) If you do not forgive, intimacy with God is not possible. Sobering, isn't it? Later, Peter talked to Christ about forgiveness, asking Him, "'Lord, how many times shall I forgive my brother or sister who sins against me? Up to seven times?' Jesus answered, 'I tell you, not seven times, but seventy-seven times.'" (Matthew 18:21-22) The message is clear. We cannot quantify forgiveness. We are to always forgive, and it will always be beneficial.

Jesus then went on to tell the disciples a story about a wicked servant who, while being forgiven by his master for a huge debt he owed, refused to forgive a fellow servant of a much smaller debt owed to him. When the master heard about this, he demanded that the wicked servant be tortured until he could pay back everything he originally owed. Then, to hammer home the message, Christ said these piercing words: "This is how my heavenly Father

Taming Anger: The Explosive Hijacker

will treat each of you unless you forgive your brother from your heart."

Indeed, forgiveness is important to the Lord, as these other passages affirm:

- "And when you stand praying, if you hold anything against anyone, forgive them, so that your Father in heaven may forgive your sins." (Mark 11:25)
- "Do not judge, and you will not be judged. Do not condemn, and you will not be condemned. Forgive, and you will be forgiven." (Luke 6:37)
- "If they sin against you seven times in a day and seven times come back to you saying, 'I repent,' you must forgive them." (Luke 17:4)
- "Bear with each other and forgive one another if any of you has a grievance against someone. Forgive as the Lord forgave you." (Colossians 3:13)

I talked to a man on my show who shared how he had to forgive the drunk driver that killed his only daughter. I asked him, "What do mean you *had* to forgive him?" He said, "I know it's the right thing to do. I had to forgive him for my own spiritual and mental health, but mostly, it's what my daughter would have wanted." Yet what do you do when you've been so deeply hurt—by a spouse or ex-spouse, one of your children, a parent, a close friend—that you struggle to let go of your anger?

1. **Be clear on *what* needs to be forgiven.** The clearer you are concerning the offenses you have experienced from another person, the more precise

you can be when you begin to go through the process of forgiveness. Donna and I do this when an angry word comes between us, and on those occasions when we don't, a restless night of sleep usually gets us back on track. Anger separates and distance grows, but consistent forgiveness closes the gap and brings us closer together.

2. **Acknowledge your feelings.** By acknowledging your feelings, you are helping to clarify your thoughts and connect your heart to your head, beginning to take the process to the next step. Since the forgiveness process may include confrontation and accountability, the setting of appropriate boundaries, or grieving, it may be helpful to seek the help of your pastor, a mentor, or a counselor to assist you.

3. **Speak, write, or in some tangible way articulate your forgiveness.** Speaking forgiveness out loud not only declares what you are thinking, but actually hearing it further solidifies in your mind the decision to forgive. Even a tangible ceremony can be helpful. I once spoke at a marriage conference up in the mountains, and we went through the process points of forgiveness and holding grudges. Later that evening, I had a closing session, which happened to be around the campfire with the other couples. I had each person pick up a piece of straw that was on the ground which represented the offense and hurt they felt. Next, I asked them to consider God's forgiveness and to be willing to forgive the other

person. Then, if they chose, I directed them to take that piece of straw to the campfire, toss it in, and watch it burn. That simple act was symbolic of what God does with our offenses as they turn to vapor before Him. We need to leave the offenses there and not take them home with us. It was powerful.
4. **Don't confuse forgiveness with accountability.** Forgiveness is something you freely give to another person. The consequences of their actions, however, is their responsibility. In parenting, we forgive our children for disobedience, but the intentional parent doesn't then jump in to protect their child from the logical or natural consequences of that disobedience. If a teenager, for example, is irresponsible with the family car, the consequence is obvious and necessary for proper training: they lose the right to drive the car.

Make a Bold Move: DO the next right one thing.
1. Think of the name of one person you need to forgive.
2. Identify the offense that you need to forgive. Be specific.
3. Envision that offense being burned away by the light of God's love and forgiveness.
4. Take joy in how that makes you feel.

WHY IS FORGIVENESS IMPORTANT?

John 3:16 is a verse you've no doubt committed to memory, but read it again like it's the first time: "For God so loved the world that he gave his one and only Son, that whoever believes in him shall not perish but have eternal life." God did the forgiving long before you did the repenting. This model of forgiveness is vital in that it sets the stage for three key points you should remember when dealing with someone who has wronged you and is unrepentant.

First, even though God initiated forgiveness, it still didn't change the relationship between Himself and His creation. You must accept that forgiveness in order for that to happen. In other words, even though God gave His Son to forgive you of all your sins, you must still recognize and accept it—and that acceptance brings the change in the relationship between you and God. The same is true of the unrepentant person in your life. Your sole responsibility is to forgive. It's up to them to accept it.

> **God did the forgiving long before you did the repenting.**

Second, forgiveness is something you can do regardless of the circumstances. God knew in advance of Christ's death and resurrection that millions of people over the ages would reject His incredible act of love…but He did it anyway.

Third, you can forgive even if the other person could care less or is no longer alive. At a conference about forgiveness, I was asked by an older woman about a long deceased parent that had abused her throughout her childhood. "He's been dead for years, but I am still angry at him," she said. "How do I forgive when he's not here?" For many reasons, including death, it may not be possible or advisable to speak with the person who has wronged you. I suggested that she write her deceased father a letter expressing her hurt and pain, then read her letter out loud to her father, perhaps even at his graveside if possible. Next, I directed her to forgive her father, commit her hurt and anger to God, and ask Him to heal her wounded heart and give her freedom. It's never too late to forgive someone.

WHAT ABOUT FORGIVING OURSELVES?

In the end, forgiveness is actually something you give to *yourself* because it brings you freedom from hijacked emotions.

Jesus taught a powerful parable in the book of Luke, spoken when He was visiting the home of a Pharisee named Simon. "'Two people owed money to a certain moneylender. One owed him five hundred denarii, and the other fifty. Neither of them had the money to pay him back, so he forgave the debts of both. Now which of them will love him more?' Simon replied, 'I suppose the one who had the bigger debt forgiven.' 'You have judged correctly,' Jesus said. Then he turned toward the woman and said to Simon, 'Do you see this woman? I came into your house. You did not give me any water for my feet, but she wet my feet with her tears and wiped them with her hair. You did not give me a kiss, but this woman, from the time I entered, has not stopped kissing my feet. You did not put oil on my head, but she has poured perfume on my feet. Therefore, I tell you, her many sins have been forgiven—as her great love has shown. But whoever has been forgiven little loves little.'" (Luke 7:41-47)

This account reminds you how important it is to look at what God has done for you by taking your eyes off your anger at yourself by focusing instead on His love and forgiveness for you.

Here are three things you can do that'll help you better understand and appreciate God's forgiveness of your sins so that you can forgive yourself:

1. List all the things that God has forgiven you for. This may seem self-focusing, but it's not because this list does not represent your past failures or shortcomings, but instead God's incredible faithfulness to forgive you of those things again and again. Then ask yourself: "Why am I holding onto feelings of anger about my past sin when God clearly isn't?"

2. Recognize that when you fail to forgive yourself you are committing an unnecessary act of self-focus that not only dishonors God's forgiveness of you but also actually derails the positive impact that forgiveness should be having on your life. Instead of living in freedom as God intends, you're still placing yourself in spiritual bondage to a sin that already has been forgiven and taken away from you by God: "As far as the east is from the west, so far has he removed our transgressions from us" (Psalm 103:12).

3. If you haven't already done so, memorize and live this verse every day: "If we confess our sins, he is

faithful and just and will forgive us our sins and purify us from all unrighteousness" (1 John 1:9).

Make a Bold Move: DECLARE who's in charge of your emotions.

1. Think of one thing you've said or done in anger that you now regret. Don't allow Satan to beat you up with regret and guilt.
2. Intentional living will give you freedom as you pray and do what you can to take responsibility for your attitude or actions.
3. Envision yourself being forgiven by God and released from that guilt.
4. Take a moment to consider how that will make you feel.

As much as anger can lead to hijacked emotions, fear can be just as detrimental. But it, too, can be dealt with as you apply God's power, love, and mindset to your most pressing anxieties and concerns and make bold moves in response.

Bold Move Questions: DECLUTTER your emotions.

1. What have I felt angry about in the past several days?

___

2. What do I believe is the root issue of that anger?

___

3. How should I respond to that root issue to properly address my expressions of anger?

___

Bold Move Questions: DECIDE who's in charge of your emotions.

1. What injustice makes me angry? Why?

___

2. What can I do intentionally to respond to that anger in a godly way?

___

3. How can I try to envision the results of my response.

4. How does that make me feel?

Bold Move Questions: DO the next right one thing.

1. Whose name pops into my mind whenever I hear a message about forgiveness?

2. What emotion has hijacked my life since their offense?

3. What is the next right one thing to do?

4. How does that make me feel?

Bold Move Questions: DECLARE who's in charge of your emotions.

1. In what ways is regret or guilt a problem in my life?

2. How have I accepted responsibility for my words or actions?

3. Do I believe God forgives sin? Do I feel forgiven? Why or why not?

4. How does that make me feel?

5

Tearing Down the Walls of Anxiety and Fear

There's a healthy and unhealthy response to every fear. God designed our brains to respond with the healthy physiological response of "fight or flight" whenever we are posed with a situation that either prepares our bodies to stay and fight or readies it to flee.

For instance, one hot summer day in Tucson, I boarded a flight scheduled to take me to a conference back east. The plane was packed, and as I settled back in seat 12D, I wondered how many of the passengers were looking forward to reaching their destinations to escape from the 100-plus degree heat outside. I reached up, adjusted the air conditioner vent so the cool air hit me just right, and settled in for what I assumed was going to be another uneventful flight.

Fear often arrives when you least expect it. In this case, it happened just at takeoff when the jet's front wheels were off the ground and the craft was just getting ready to start its ascent.

BOOM!

At that moment, one of the two engines—the one on my side of the plane—exploded. The plane shook violently, and everyone fell into an eerie silence, expecting the worst. We didn't know what would happen. My first thought was we were already too far down the runway, so the pilot was either going to take off with one engine and crash, or he was going to run it off the end of the runway into a ditch. Neither option was good. It was a helpless, out-of-control feeling. I thought of Donna and our children and grandchildren, and, of course, I prayed.

Thankfully, the pilot was able to bring the plane back to the ground and screech to a halt at the end of the runaway. His heroic performance was recognized by thunderous, appreciative applause. Sitting right in front of me was a pilot from the same airline who was transporting to another airport. He looked at me.

"We were lucky," he said.

"I think it was more than that," I responded. "God had His hand in this today."

When the engine blew, I experienced a healthy "fight or flight" response to fear. My mind and body were readied for action even though there was no one to fight and I had nowhere to flight. I was trapped along with every other passenger. It was all up to the pilot. It was only as the plane taxied back toward the gate that my heart rate and thinking returned to normal levels as the fear dissipated. That's the way healthy fear should work. I faced a legitimate threat and my response fueled my tank to take the necessary action.

THE DIFFERENCE BETWEEN ANXIETY AND FEAR

We use anxiety and fear interchangeably to describe emotions, but they are slightly different. Both impact us physically and emotionally, and both cause the "fight or flight" response to kick in. Fear is typically triggered by an actual threat of some impending danger. For example, "I'm fearful of being in this tall building," or "I'm afraid of the approaching tornado," or "I'm scared of falling down the back steps in the dark." Fear increases as danger approaches and decreases as it leaves.

Both anxiety and fear can hijack your emotional life.

Anxiety, however, is more of a general feeling that something is not right in your world. For example, "I'm anxious about the future of the economy," or "I'm worried about my health," or "I'm anxious about making a presentation next month at work." Ongoing anxiety, unlike situational fear, is more likely to create feelings of restlessness, fatigue, muscle tension, and difficulty concentrating. I once read that over 40 million American adults struggle with serious anxiety.

Both anxiety and fear can hijack your emotional life. Here are three things to help:

1. **Let it go!** In 1 Peter 5:7, the Bible tells you to "cast all your anxiety on him because he cares for you."
2. **Just breathe.** Job, a man who certainly knew something about fear and anxiety, declared, "The Spirit of God has made me; the breath of the Almighty gives me life." (Job 33:4)
3. **Change your focus from your fear and anxiety.** In Luke 12:29-31, Jesus said, "Do not set your heart on what you will eat or drink; do not worry about it. For the pagan world runs after all such things, and your Father knows that you need them. But seek his kingdom, and these things will be given to you as well."

DON'T GET HIJACKED BY ANXIETY AND FEAR

It's when "fight or flight" gets stuck in the "on" position that unhealthy things start to happen. A constant state of anxiety and fear does strange things to people and can lead to all sorts of negative results physically, emotionally, spiritually, and relationally. It draws content out of our lives like hot water draws tea out of a tea bag, bringing out behaviors that aren't typical. Constant anxiety and fear will wear you out.

This is especially true in relationships because unhealthy anxiety and fear, like anger, creates a barrier to trust where intimacy simply isn't possible. Fear-based self-talk in marriage can ask some alarming questions:

- "Does he love me?"
- "She had an affair last year. Is she being faithful to me now?"
- "Do I measure up to what he expects?"

A marriage built on this kind of anxiety and fear will eventually crumble or at least sink into a dip. People who like to please others are often drawn to a spouse who appears at first to be confident, controlled, and focused, but may actually be critical and controlling. An anxious or fearful person builds a wall around themselves for self-protection. Eventually, that anxiety and fear, masked in busyness, control, or anger, gnaws away at the foundation of the relationship until the marriage collapses under the weight of it all.

In my book, *Starved for Affection*, I wrote that "most marriages don't disintegrate suddenly or without reason. Over time, layer upon layer of often unintentional carelessness causes most marital problems. Just as lack of food will lead to physical starvation, the lack of proper care and feeding of the emotional well-being of your marriage will likely result in all sorts of troubling outcomes."[1] When emotions such as unhealthy anxiety and fear get hijacked, you and your spouse are constantly on edge, self-protection increases, walls go up, and intimacy drops. I found a poem by an unknown author called "Walls" that poignantly concludes, "For when love dies, it is not in a moment of angry battle, nor when fiery bodies lose their heat. It lies panting, exhausted, expiring at the bottom of a wall it could not scale."[2] Tearing down the walls of anxiety and fear will allow your marriage to thrive.

In relationships and life in general, unhealthy anxiety and fear steals your motivation and excitement for the future. It gets us out of the way of oncoming traffic, but it doesn't get us to our destination. It causes us to lock our doors at night, but it doesn't give us restful sleep. Unhealthy anxiety and fear doesn't add to or multiply anything in your life. It only subtracts and divides.

> **An anxious or fearful person builds a wall around themselves for self-protection.**

That was the case for Jackie when she called in to my show. "My fear is death, the whole process," she revealed, "the physical process of dying and loved ones dying around me."

I asked, "Do you know Christ, Jackie?" She replied that she did. "Alright, so you know intellectually as a Christian that if you were to die, or if people who know Christ were to die, where they would be spiritually?"

"Yes."

"Have you been around death?" I asked.

"I've actually had several people close to me pass away," Jackie said, "and I don't know if it traumatized me in some way, but I feel like I can't deal with it."

I affirmed that death is indeed traumatic. "Did you have experiences with death as a child?"

"Yes," she said. "Around the age of five or so my grandmother died. She was like a mother to me."

"You're still processing these losses in your life, aren't you?"

"Yes."

I then exhorted her that she did not have to stay trapped in her unhealthy anxiety and fear of death. I quoted Philippians 1:21 to her ("For to me, to live is Christ and to die is gain.") and then told her, "Even though we don't rush to death, we know there's a gain to be experienced for the follower of Christ." I knew it would take time, but I hoped she would eventually be able to realign her mindset with Scripture, along with its reminder of God's love and power over death, would free her from that hijacked emotion. I knew that how she saw fear of death as a heart experience might be difficult.

> **Unhealthy anxiety and fear doesn't add to or multiply anything in your life. It only subtracts and divides.**

Patterns of thinking can be very sticky. As the Bible instructs us, we are to "take captive every thought to make it obedient to Christ." (2 Corinthians 10:5) That requires intentionally creating new habits of thinking, for that's the only way your emotions, especially with traumatic experiences involving death, will be moved to the heart. Often, the help of a counselor, a pastor, or a combination of the two is necessary to walk through those times.

Unhealthy anxiety and fear can also make you feel insecure and unsafe. That's what happened with Anne from

Washington. She called in to tell me her concern. "I got hurt," she said, "and now my anger has turned into fear."

"When you say you're angry, what are you angry about?" I asked.

"Well, I *was* angry. My husband hurt me with his words and actions, but we've been working through it," she clarified. "He's been in counseling for six months."

"So, what do you feel anxious about?" I pressed.

"I'm paranoid that I'm going to get hurt again because the focus is coming off of him and changing. Now it's on me not getting over it. And it's a hard road."

"It's also a road that is reality," I responded, "particularly if you're in an intimate relationship where one person hurts another person, which God never intended and should never happen. The only way that is going to heal is for you to feel safe. You've got to be in a place where you feel able to grow and deal with this in a healthy way." I added, "If you're not feeling that, then you shouldn't lay guilt on yourself. You need to say, 'I just don't feel safe,' and seek the help that you need to make sure that not only do you feel safe, but that you really *are* safe."

If you've experienced emotional pain because of death or a marital issue, healing requires a *safe place* emotionally and physically. It's critical. Let's say after a surgery on your hip you're very tentative walking around because you feel like you might fall. The reality is you could indeed fall. It's not only anxiety and fear, but a legitimate concern. Until you start feeling more confident in your ability to stand and walk on your own, you may need to take precautions such as using a walker or having someone walk with you to catch you if you fall. But, as you realize you're getting stronger, you start to regain your footing. This can't happen, though, unless you're safe emotionally and physically.

When my children were younger, I was a fairly overprotective father and was concerned for their safety—sometimes a bit too much. When Andrea was about eight years old, I saw her walking across the room wildly swinging a pencil in her right hand. My immediate fear was that she might hurt herself, so I said, "Andrea, don't poke your eye out with that pencil." My wife, Donna, playfully asked, "Why would she want to poke her eye out?" Unhealthy fear can cause us to say and do irrational things. Andrea and I still have fun with that incident. When I speak to her on the phone as she's serving in missions in West Africa, I'll sometimes close our conversation with, "Don't poke your eye out." It's my way of saying, "Be safe."

We receive comments from people about anxiety and fear all the time through our ministry comment phone line as well as our Facebook page. Here are some things people have shared with us:

- Kelda said, "My biggest anxiety and fear in life by far is speaking in front of people, but I think that's probably a fear most people have."
- Jenny shared, "My anxiety and fear is that harm could come to my children. I know I have to let go and let God, but just knowing the world is out there and they're in it is scary enough."
- Hector told us, "I think my biggest anxiety and fear would be failing as a Christian man. I wasn't brought

up in a Christ-centered home, so I've had to learn many lessons the hard way. I do have to point out that if we have Jesus, we shouldn't be anxious or fearful, but it is still there sometimes anyway."

Unhealthy anxiety and fear can lead to bad decisions. Anxiety and fear cause a drowning victim to fight the rescuer. Anxiety and fear of rejection can cause people to marry the wrong person even though red flags are flying or to stay in an abusive relationship for fear of being alone. Anxiety and fear cause distrust. It can cause leaders to throw in the towel and give up too soon. Anxiety and fear keep us from connecting with people we need and who need us.

Perhaps worst of all, anxiety and fear can prevent us from getting closer to Christ. Once you've taken the first big step to acknowledge your unhealthy anxiety and fear, God will help you and be with you. It's a process of intentionally growing in your faith so that you can consistently experience His presence.

I am convinced that God has a solution for whatever anxiety and fear you have in your life today, but if you are not intentional in embracing the truth of God's love for you in the midst of it, you will remain trapped in a chaotic, frightening kind of a life—one where you feel like the plane could go down at any moment. That's no way to live.

There's freedom for you, and it's found in 2 Timothy 1:7, which declares, "For God has not given us the spirit of fear; but of power and of love and of a sound mind." (KJV) Those three concepts—power, love, and a sound mind—are a triangle of strength for those of us who have a relationship with Christ. They can help us to deal with unhealthy anxiety and fear.

POWER

When I was in Michigan for a board meeting for Youth Haven, I stayed in their large lodge building, which was virtually empty on the night I arrived. It was a hot, muggy, stormy July evening, and in the middle of the night, there was a power failure which caused the air conditioning to shut off. I woke up as the room began to overheat and realized that none of the lights worked and the entire building was dark and silent. Only emergency lights dimly lit the path in the hallways, and all I could hear was the blaring of a distant emergency alarm. Two hours later, the power came back on, the air conditioners started, and the ceiling fans started to once again circulate the air. In an instant, the eeriness was replaced with light, life, and cool air because the power was back on!

> **I am convinced that God has a solution for whatever anxiety and fear you have in your life today.**

It's easy to take God's power for granted, but if His power went out for even a minute, the darkness and deafening silence would be overwhelming. Paul reminds us that our strength to defeat anxiety and fear is not our own but comes from God. "Finally, be strong in the Lord and in his mighty power." (Ephesians 6:10)

As Christians, we have the opportunity to tap into the source of true power through our relationship with God via the Holy Spirit. Tapping into that power releases your spiritual gifts. Becoming confident in God's power gives you assurance to be bold and live the intentional life. Trying to do things in your own power will leave you exhausted, anxious, and fearful, yet as you practice using His Spirit of power given to you as a gift from God, anxiety and fear will begin to lose its control over your life.

Make a Bold Move: DEVELOP a plan of action to respond to emotional triggers.

Here are three ways you can tap into God's power right now and any time you need it:

1. Prayer–Ask the Holy Spirit for the power to face your anxieties and fears and defeat them.
2. Meditate on Scripture–Memorize these verses and spend time thinking about these promises.
    - "The Lord is my light and my salvation—whom shall I fear? The Lord is the stronghold of my life—of whom shall I be afraid?" (Psalm 27:1)
    - "Whoever listens to me will live in safety and be at ease, without fear of harm." (Proverbs 1:33)
    - "Come to me, all you who are weary and burdened, and I will give you rest." (Matthew 11:28)

3. Act in faith–Start moving forward, trusting God, and facing your anxieties and fears by not backing down.

LOVE

Biblical love is action focused. Taking action will build your confidence as you overcome the hijacked emotions of anxiety and fear. The opposite of anxiety and fear is confidence. As Proverbs 14:26 tells us, "In the fear of the Lord is strong confidence: and his children shall have a place of refuge." (KJV)

We don't fight one negative emotion with another negative emotion, but with intentional love in action that draws strength from the Holy Spirit in order to act. This process takes our minds off our anxieties and fears and places it on doing the next right one thing. For example:

- If you are anxious and fearful about meeting people who are different than you, be intentional and get to know one new person this week that isn't in your circle of friends.
- If you are anxious and fearful about your finances, get with your spouse, pray, and take action to put together a simple spending plan and follow it.
- If you are anxious and fearful about what's happening with your children, pray for them daily and ask God to build a hedge of protection around them.
- If you are anxious and fearful about your health, get a physical, ask your doctor what you can do to improve your health, and act on it daily.

The characteristics of love are clearly spelled out in the Bible in 1 Corinthians 13. Read and follow the behaviors of love recorded specifically in verses 4 through 8: "Love is patient, love is kind. It does not envy, it does not boast, it is not proud. It does not dishonor others, it is not self-seeking, it is not easily angered, it keeps no record of wrongs. Love does not delight in evil but rejoices with the truth. It always protects, always trusts, always hopes, always perseveres. Love never fails."

Now, insert yourself into these behaviors of love and begin to see yourself acting these out to come against your unhealthy anxieties and fears:

I am patient. I am kind. I do not envy. I do not boast. I am not proud. I am not going to dishonor others. I am not self-seeking. I am not easily angered. I keep no record of wrongs. I do not delight in evil but rejoice with the truth. I always protect, always trust, always hope, always persevere. Because love never fails—I never fail.

Make a Bold Move: DEVELOP a plan of action to respond to emotional triggers.

Take one of these attributes of love and practice it in all your relationships for the next 30 days.

1. Intentionally smile at people.
2. Be intentionally friendly and helpful.
3. Be intentionally generous with praise.
4. Be intentionally thoughtful of the opinions of others.

Tearing Down the Walls of Anxiety and Fear

A SOUND MIND

The key to a sound mind is relying on and cooperating with the Holy Spirit to retain your discipline. During times of unhealthy anxiety and fear, you can overreact or underreact. Self-discipline provides a steady hand that tells you the truth about your situation.

"I can make it!"

"God is with me."

"There is something I can do to make things better."

"This won't last forever."

It was a lack of disciplined thinking that hijacked Jim's emotions, leading him to consistently overreact to his wife whenever she tried to express how she felt about almost any issue going on in their family or marriage. He took her assertions personally, interpreting them as an attack on him, which wasn't his wife's intention. Because of Jim's own personal insecurities, his immature responses to his wife typically led to arguments. That only made everything worse.

> **You can affect your tomorrow by what you choose to think about today.**

Finding freedom from unhealthy anxiety and fear or any other hijacked emotion takes two things: telling yourself the truth and then acting on that truth daily. In my book, *The Power of One Thing*, I shared these insights on how to manage your thinking.[3]

1. Create your own thinking list. "Get a piece of paper

or your journal and list topics that represent the deepest concerns in your life. What matters most to you? ... Only you can determine what those are."
2. Capture your thoughts for personal growth and prayer. "Write down your thoughts to help you order and organize them. One advantage of journaling is that it takes all the jumbled thoughts in your mind and forces them out of the pen—one word at a time."
3. Schedule time to think every day. "What you thought about yesterday is shaping your life today. That means you can affect your tomorrow by what you choose to think about today. The list you create is a great starting point."
4. Take control of your thinking. "Neglecting to schedule time is one reason many people don't think productively."

Self-discipline starts with our thinking and ends with our behavior. We can have a sound mind in the face of unhealthy anxiety and fear when we exercise self-discipline.

Make a Bold Move: DECIDE who's in charge of your emotions.

1. Make a "thinking list" and have it ready the next time you have an extra hour just to be quiet and think about the important things in your life.
2. Start a journal to capture your thoughts and feelings. You will notice patterns

of both, which should give insight into your emotions.

DON'T STAY STUCK

One of the best ways to deal with anxiety and fear is to become proactive and solution-focused. Refuse to just sit there and be stuck with it. Not surprisingly, anxiety and fear breed more anxiety and fear. Any emotion tends to feed upon itself and build if we let it go long enough. It's just the way it works.

Why is worry so debilitating? We want to control something but feel like we can't, and that makes us afraid. At those times when irrational anxiety and fear have a hold on me, I will ask myself, "What's the worst thing that can happen to me?" Ultimately, it's that I get to go home to heaven, the eternal destination Christ has called us to possess. That's a good thing. Therefore, whatever it is that you fear is in God's hands. He knows about it and He controls it. We can fully trust in Him for the outcome.

Family Life Radio artist Zach Williams sings a song entitled, "Fear is a Liar." In it, he exhorts, *Fear, he is a liar / He will take your breath / Stop you in your steps / Fear, he is a liar / He will rob your rest / Steal your happiness / Cast your fear in the fire / 'Cause fear, he is a liar.* That's the truth. Anxiety and fear will hold you down, pull you back, lay you flat, and discourage you from taking intentional action for good. Don't let anxiety and fear do that to you. Tear down its walls using God's triangle of strength—power, love, and a sound mind!

Bold Move Questions: DEVELOP a plan of action to respond to emotional triggers.

1. Do I truly live by faith in everything? If not, why not?

   _____

   _____

2. Do I pray enough about my emotional triggers? Write a short prayer below, asking God to help you overcome emotional triggers in your life.

   _____

   _____

3. Do I meditate on scripture to help me manage my emotions? Write how each of the verses below speak to you?
   - "The Lord is my light and my salvation—whom shall I fear? The Lord is the stronghold of my life—of whom shall I be afraid?" (Psalm 27:1)
   - "Whoever listens to me will live in safety and be at ease, without fear of harm." (Proverbs 1:33)
   - "Come to me, all you who are weary and burdened, and I will give you rest." (Matthew 11:28)

   _____

   _____

Tearing Down the Walls of Anxiety and Fear

Bold Move Questions: DEVELOP a plan of action to respond to emotional triggers.

1. Who do I need to smile at more often? Why?

___

2. With whom do I need to be more friendly and helpful? Why?

___

3. With whom do I need to be more generous with my praise? Why?

___

4. Who needs me to be more thoughtful of their opinions, especially when I disagree? Why?

___

Bold Move Questions: DECIDE who's in charge of your emotions.

1. In addition to the list from *The Power of One Thing*, what else can I do to create more self-discipline in my life?

   _____

   _____

2. What can I do intentionally to respond to unhealthy fear in a godly way?

   _____

   _____

3. How does it make me feel as I envision the positive results of my response?

   _____

   _____

6

How to Get Through an Emotional Dip

If you live in a hilly area like I do, you're familiar with them—but they can still catch you by surprise, even if you know they're inevitable. You'll be driving along, nice and level, and then all of a sudden—*swoop!* A dip in the road plummets you downward, taking your stomach with it, only to quickly rise upward and send you along your way until the next one takes you on a similar ride. It's much like a mini roller coaster ride.

Life, too, has emotional dips, but unlike the ones in the road, they can last anywhere from a few hours to a few days or even weeks at a time. Regardless of their length or severity, you have to be on guard to make sure your emotions don't hijack your contentment when you're in them.

I hit an emotional dip in 1994 when my dad died. Even though he had been ill for several years, his death hit me hard. Suddenly, his encouraging words were silenced.

Freedom from Hijacked Emotions

His infectious positivity was gone. His counsel became only memories from past conversations. Even though I knew his spiritual life and his Heavenly home was safely secured, the hole left by his absence led to one of the most severe emotional dips in my life.

The first days after his death were kept busy with funeral planning, traveling, and spending time with family. I was too preoccupied to think about the loss much less grieve it. Then, three weeks after his death, I woke up in the middle of the night and sped into the dip at full speed. My emotional guard was lowered and the emotional ooze I had stuffed away instantly erupted. My dip lasted for the next several weeks, and even though I knew I was experiencing normal grief, and intellectually recognized I wouldn't always feel that way, it was hard to accept. It became a time of severe testing. *Is my faith true? Does it work in this time of hurt?*

As I reflected on my father's final weeks, I recalled that he'd had 27 different surgeries, and every time he had recovered. So, I'd started to believe that no matter how ill he was, he was going to come back. It wasn't until he didn't that I realized I needed to trust that God knew what He was doing. There was a time and season for everything. That was the time for my dad.

During my emotional dip, I moved from a theoretical concept of God's sovereignty to acceptance of His sovereignty, which allowed me to accept my father's death. It wasn't easy, and I was thankful for Donna's patience during that time. Since then, we have been through other deep losses, and my understanding of God's sovereignty is more immediate, but that first time was a wake-up call.

How to Get Through an Emotional Dip

Emotional dips, even difficult ones caused by the loss of a loved one, are normal to life—but staying in the dip isn't. How can we avoid lingering in the dip of a hijacked emotion and get through it to the other side?

Like driving through a dip in the road, moving forward will provide the momentum you need to get out of the dip and proceed in life. It's interesting how some people can face discouragement, defeat, or rejection, go into an emotional dip, and get stuck, while others persevere, overcome, and press onward. Remember the classic TV show *I Love Lucy?* Lucille Ball, the queen of comedy, dominated those early years of television because of how she was so physical with her comedy and the way she connected with people. Yet it might surprise you to learn that Lucille Ball was actually dismissed from drama school. She was told she was wasting her time and too shy to put her best foot forward. Michael Jordan was cut from his high school basketball team and went home disillusioned and discouraged, but we all know how that worked out. Thomas Edison's teacher told him he was too stupid to learn anything and that he should go into a field where he might succeed by virtue of his pleasant personality. Walt Disney was fired from a newspaper and told he lacked imagination and had no original ideas.

> **The thing about these dips is you can't go around them.**

We've all had times when things went wrong or differently than expected, and we went into an emotional dip. The thing about these dips is you can't go around them.

You can't go over them. You have to go through them. It's *how* you go through them that determines when—and if—you keep moving and have the momentum to come out.

Let's look at some of the different kinds of emotional dips you can experience and examine how you can successfully avoid hijacked emotions when making your way through them.

REFLECTIVE DIPS

Early in our marriage, Donna and I were asked to take on a huge responsibility for a young couple. We moved 125 miles from Jackson to Midland, Michigan to build and launch a 100,000-watt FM radio station, hire professional staff, and create programming for a new 24-hour-per-day Christian station. It was the third one in the fledgling Family Life Radio network, covering a large portion of central Michigan. Not long after successfully starting the station, we were called back to the ministry headquarters in Jackson, and I was asked to be national program director for Family Life Radio. Over the next few years, two of our three children were born, and we helped direct the move of our entire network headquarters from Michigan to Tucson, Arizona where we had

> **It may be that the dip you're in is the result of not understanding God's intention for your life.**

just purchased another radio station from cowboy singer, songwriter, and actor Gene Autry.

It was a lot for a young 20-something couple to be given, but we accepted every challenge. As we settled into our new home in Tucson, we were happy, God was blessing us, and life was good. But I slowly started to slip into a dip—a reflective dip. When I turned 31 years old, I started to think, *Now what? We've done all these things, so what's next?* It was a time of reflection and exploration, which is not uncommon when we get into our thirties and forties. At the time, I was halfway through my college education and had a strong, unmet desire to help people. I loved radio, but I wanted to be even more personally engaged in guiding others in their emotional, spiritual, and relational lives.

God used that dip, and it was during that season that I made decisions that completely altered the course of my life. By the time I was 33, I was back in college at the University of Arizona. Two years later, I completed my master's degree in counseling—something I had long wanted to achieve. Within the next 10 years, I completed my doctorate, wrote a couple of books, and launched a national radio program called *Parent Talk,* which later became *Intentional Living*. Part of coming out of the reflective dip for me involved setting new direction. In the process, I found my purpose and pursued it with passion. Reflective dips can be a gift—if you use them to become more intentional with your life.

There are two key questions to ask yourself when you're in a reflective dip.

Freedom from Hijacked Emotions

1. **Is this dip caused because I'm looking for my purpose?** It may be that the dip you're in is the result of not understanding God's intention for your life. Over the years, I've often had to encourage capable and talented staff members to leave our ministry so they could find and pursue their purpose. It wasn't because they couldn't do their job or were bad employees. It just became clear that they were square pegs trying to fit into round holes because God's intent for their lives was different and greater.
2. **Is this dip caused because I lack passion?** Passion follows purpose. It's impossible to have a lasting passion for marriage, parenting, or a career without first understanding and accepting the purpose for each. Our ministry at *Intentional Living* is all about helping people to know their purpose and passionately live it out. One reason so many marriages end in divorce is a lack of passion for the relationship resulting from not understanding God's intention for their marriage relationally, sexually, emotionally, financially, and spiritually.

Make a Bold Move: DECLUTTER your emotions.

1. When you're in a dip, expect periods of hijacked emotions to occur. Emotions happen. Don't overreact or allow your emotions to drop you further into the dip.
2. Allow the Holy Spirit to quietly give you comfort as you keep moving forward in faith.

3. Moving forward is important whenever you're in a dip. So, do the next right one thing, no matter how small it may be.

INVISIBLE DIPS

These are the ones we just don't see coming. We're going along in life, everything is going great, and then it's like the bottom falls out. Something occurs and you realize you're not where you thought you were. Invisible dips could be emotional, physical, or financial. They can happen in your faith walk or may be in your career or health. Most of the time you wonder, *How in the world did I get here?*

In 1998, I woke up in an invisible dip. To this day I don't know how I got into it, or what brought me out of it, and other than God, I don't know how I got out of it. For weeks I felt lost and aimless. I went for walks by myself, trying to figure out what was going on. I felt no direction—and no peace. My life was okay. I wasn't in any big crisis. My family was doing well. Work was fine. I just bottomed out. What I feared most was that this feeling wouldn't pass—and what worried me the most was I couldn't identify the source. I fix other people's problems, so I figured if I knew the reason, I could fix it. Later, I wondered if God had allowed me to have the experience so that I could have more empathy for people. Throughout the dip, I told myself the truth to keep me moving forward with my day-to-day life, but I think the practical thing that helped me as much as anything was exercise. I went for a long walk most every night and intentionally practiced thinking clearly, praying, and asking God for relief—and He brought it in His own time.

When you're blindsided by an invisible dip, here are a pair of important rules to follow.

1. **Press forward**. If you stop at the bottom of the dip, the inertia will make it a great deal more difficult to get you up the other side and out of the dip than it would if you kept moving forward. Remember, momentum is your friend. Start by setting small, reasonable daily goals and accomplishing them intentionally. Even though the Apostle Paul was locked away in a jail cell, he continued "to press on toward the goal." (Philippians 3:14) Sometimes we proceed quickly. Other times, it's slow. But don't stop. It may only be spending 10 minutes in a prayer of thanksgiving, going out to lunch with a friend, or taking long walks like I did, but press forward and trust God.
2. **This, too, shall pass**. Invisible dips are surprising, but they are not forever. Keep in mind that it will end. However, if you're feeling totally stuck in the dip and it's continuing to drag you down week after week, or especially if you're feeling hopeless or having thoughts of hurting yourself, please get help right away.

Make a Bold Move: DEVELOP a plan of action to respond to emotional triggers.

1. Remember, after the dip comes the hill and then level ground. The dip is hard, the hill

is tiring, but the level ground is worth the effort. Keep moving.
2. Don't miss the "lesson of the dip." We learn more in the dips of life than we do on the mountaintop. Journal your thoughts and feelings as you go through a dip.
3. Keep perspective when an invisible dip appears. It may feel overwhelming.

DEEP DIPS

Some dips are deeper than others, like you've fallen off a cliff and into a dark cavern. In the book *Team of Rivals,* Pulitzer Prize-winning American historian Doris Kearns Goodwin talks about Abraham Lincoln and the men who served with him in his cabinet from 1861 to 1865. Many of these individuals were bitter rivals. In fact, they hated the president. Yet Abraham Lincoln was such a strong and mature leader that he wanted the best people around him, even if they didn't like him or his policies. Goodwin also reveals that, when Lincoln was a young man, he met Ann Rutledge. She was Lincoln's first, and perhaps most passionate, love of his life. Later in his life, Lincoln said, "I did honestly and truly love the girl and I think often of her now."[1] When Ann was only 22 years old, a deadly fever, possibly typhoid, spread through the town of New Salem. Ann, as well as several of Lincoln's friends, perished in the epidemic. Goodwin wrote, "Elizabeth Abbell, a New Salem neighbor who had become a surrogate mother to Abraham Lincoln, claims she had 'never seen a man mourn for a companion more than he did.'" Abbell went on to say that Lincoln's melancholy deepened on dark and gloomy days, for he couldn't stand having storms beat on her grave.[2]

Perhaps you have been through that depth of despair from the loss of a child, a spouse, or your health. The reality is we cannot go through life without experiencing these deep dips, but it's in these times that we can experience the closeness of God in a dramatically significant way as He walks with us through our deep dip.

Look at David's perspective as he navigates a deep dip in His life. "You have searched me, Lord, and you know me. You know when I sit and when I rise; you perceive my thoughts from afar. You discern my going out and my lying down; you are familiar with all my ways. Before a word is on my tongue you, Lord, know it completely. You hem me in behind and before, and you lay your hand upon me. Such knowledge is too wonderful for me, too lofty for me to attain. Where can I go from your Spirit? Where can I flee from your presence? If I go up to the heavens, you are there; if I make my bed in the depths, you are there. If I rise on the wings of the dawn, if I settle on the far side of the sea, even there your hand will guide me, your right hand will hold me fast. If I say, 'Surely the darkness will hide me and the light become night around me,' even the darkness will not be dark to you; the night will shine like the day, for darkness is as light to you." (Psalm 139:1-12)

When you deal with a deep dip, here are two questions you should ask yourself.

How to Get Through an Emotional Dip

1. **Who can I talk to about what I am feeling and going through in my dip?** Deep dips are lonely places, but it is when you are in the deepest part of any dip that you need others to help you not get stuck and keep moving. Reach out. Talk to your pastor, a counselor, or a mature friend. Talking helps. It will allow you to clarify your thoughts and remind you that you are not alone. If you or someone you know is really struggling with depression or thoughts of suicide, be aware there is a national suicide prevention hotline available to you.
2. **What am I hanging onto when the dip seems to get deeper and I feel like I'm losing my grip?** In my book *Father Memories*, I shared a poem called "The Pit." When you get to the final line, the answer to this question will be clear.

A man fell into a pit and couldn't get himself out.
A SUBJECTIVE person came along and said: "I feel for you down there."
An OBJECTIVE person came along and said: "It's logical that someone would fall down there."
A MATHEMATICIAN calculated how he fell into the pit.
A NEWS REPORTER wanted the exclusive story of his pit.
A FUNDAMENTALIST said: "You deserve your pit."
An IRS MAN asked if he was paying taxes on his pit.
A SELF-PITYING person said: "You haven't seen anything until you've seen MY PIT!"
A CHARISMATIC said: "Just confess that you're not in the pit."
An OPTIMIST said: "Things could be worse!"

*A PESSIMIST said: "Things will get worse!"
JESUS, seeing the man, took him by the hand and
LIFTED HIM OUT of the pit."*[3]

Look up to God and ask Him to help you. Hang onto Him, no matter how you feel or how hopeless it seems. He will see you through and bring you out of your pit.

Make a Bold Move: DECLARE who's in charge of your emotions.

1. Allow Jesus to reach down and lift you from whatever dip you're in. He loves you and will not leave you stuck forever. Pray!
2. Find a trusted friend or counselor to walk with you. Loss of perspective is to be expected in deep dip experiences, and encouragement from someone outside the dip is helpful and hopeful.
3. Take one day at time. Don't live too far into the future or dwell on the past. The further you move from this moment, the more anxiety and fear you may experience.

ANXIOUS AND FEARFUL DIPS

There are emotional dips that can create fear in our lives. Even healthy "fight or flight" anxiety or fear can sometimes prove debilitating and even cause us to ask, "Where is God in all of this?"

I was 19 and Donna was 18 when we got married. Near the close of our newlywed year, Donna suddenly became very ill. She lost a lot of weight for no apparent reason, and as a thin person to start with, she didn't have many pounds to give away. Within just a few weeks, she withered down to a mere 98 pounds. As other scary symptoms began to appear, she continued to slip away, and doctors could not figure out what was wrong.

The worse she got, the more afraid I became. I was just a kid, a young husband, and I was gripped in a fearful dip. *Am I going to lose my bride? Is she going to die? Why is this happening to her?* Donna and I were young and had our whole lives ahead of us. It didn't make any sense that this was happening to us. Together we walked through weeks of uncertainty. Within a matter of what seemed like days, we went from the mountaintop of our honeymoon and early marriage to one of the deepest pits of our lives. At one point, I had to physically lift her into and out of the car when we went to the doctor. It was horrible.

Eventually, Donna was diagnosed with a severe thyroid problem—and after surgery, she started to improve. Once we had a plan of action, we were thrilled and relieved, and Donna has remained healthy ever since, managing her thyroid with medication. That dip was one of those early moments in our marriage that helped me recognize that we needed to grow up. Life was not always going to be a honeymoon. There would be challenges, and we had to be prepared. Don't waste a fearful dip. Use it to grow. It may be painful at times, but it can be a gift to help you learn, just as Donna and I did. Her spiritual disposition is to never give up. She is more patient and even keeled. My tendency is to try to fix things, so this dip didn't cause me to lose faith or blame God. Instead, I had to learn that I can't control things. That's still an issue I wrestle with, and I'm making progress year after year.

If an anxious or fearful dip has you by the throat today, take action. Apply the advice shared in the previous chapter, as well as these two tips.

1. **Focus on the opposites of anxiety and fear.** Proverbs 3:25-26 exhorts you to "have no fear of sudden disaster or of the ruin that overtakes the wicked, for the Lord will be at your side and will keep your foot from being snared." That should give you *confidence*. Mark 4:35-41 tells of the time Jesus was on a boat with the disciples and was asleep when a powerful storm threatened to sink the vessel. "Teacher, don't you care if we drown?" they pled. Jesus got up, rebuked the wind and said to the waves, "Quiet! Be still!" Suddenly, it was completely calm. He said to His disciples, "Why are you so afraid? Do you still have no faith?" They asked one another, "Who is this? Even the wind and the waves obey him!" That should give you *faith*.

2. **Quiet your anxious and fearful mind.** I have found that physical and spiritual quietness slows down my anxious and fearful thinking. My mother was a worrier. My dad wasn't. Whenever my mom got worked up about something, he asked her, "Dorothy, what is the worst thing that could happen?" It brought her and our family back to both confidence and faith in Christ.

Make a Bold Move: DECLARE who's in charge of your emotions.
1. When you're in a fearful dip, focus on solvable problems and give the rest to God.
2. When you're in an anxious dip, intentionally separate what is "real" from those anxious thoughts that are of your own making.
3. Do the next right one thing over the next 30 days to increase your confidence and decrease anxiety and fear.

FATIGUE DIPS

Elijah's encounter with the prophets of Baal on Mount Carmel is an example of the discouragement cycle many people experience when going into and coming out of a fatigue dip. Elijah was a prophet of God living in a time of great disobedience in the lives of the children of Israel. Not only were they not honoring the Lord, they had become followers of the prophets of Baal. Prompted by God, Elijah commanded King Ahab to summon the people from all over Israel to meet him at Mount Carmel. While hosting a tour to Israel, I had the privilege of standing near where Elijah stood. I taught the story from 1 Kings. In chapter 18 verse 21, Elijah challenged the people, "'How long will you waver between two opinions? If the Lord is God, follow him; but if Baal is God, follow him.' But the people said nothing."

At this point of the account, Elijah was in the first stage of the three stages of discouragement: a high level of commitment. He was standing on Mount Carmel with 450 prophets of Baal with the Lord at His side, and he was excited about the assignment God had given him to confront the people about their disobedience.

Have you ever been enthusiastic about a commitment? "I'm going to take better care of my health." "I'm going to start taking care of my finances." "I'm going to be a better spouse." Sometimes we get that way at the start of each new year when we make resolutions to better ourselves in some way or another. It's wonderful, and optimism flows.

> **I have found that physical and spiritual quietness slows down my anxious and fearful thinking.**

It certainly did for Elijah. He challenged the prophets of Baal, even taunted them, pleading with them to call upon Baal to light the fire under their sacrificial altar, but nothing happened. "Shout louder!" Elijah told them. "Surely he is a god! Perhaps he is deep in thought, or busy, or traveling. Maybe he is sleeping and must be awakened." (1 Kings 18:27) In the end, Elijah called down the power of the one true God who consumed the altar, and then he had Baal's prophets slaughtered. He was confident, bold, and even audacious.

But, after King Ahab told Jezebel all that Elijah had done and how he had executed all the prophets of Baal, Jezebel sent a message to Elijah. "May the gods deal with me, be it ever so severely, if by this time tomorrow I do not make your life like that of one of them." (1 Kings 19:2) Nothing like a good old-fashioned death threat to ruin your day, right? But Elijah had just called on the power of God and seen it mightily manifested. Surely he wouldn't be fazed.

He was—and then some. Suddenly, the prophet of God was afraid. Even more, verse 3 says he "ran for his life" and then, somewhere deep in the wilderness, exclaimed, "'I have had enough, Lord,' he said. 'Take my life; I am no better than my ancestors.' Then he lay down under the bush and fell asleep." (1 Kings 19:4-5)

What happened? Elijah fell into a fatigue dip. He was exhausted—the second stage of the three stages of discouragement—and the same thing can happen to us. I'm convinced that most of us sincerely want to be intentional in our faith, relationships, health, finances, and work. Yet it's easy to become weary in doing good (Galatians 6:9). I find that my fatigue dips usually come right after a high point in my life. Pastor, author, educator, and radio preacher Charles Swindoll, in his book, *Growing Strong in The Seasons of Life*, cites three of many reasons why a Christian can become weary and quotes Scripture to go with each one: waiting ("I am exhausted from crying for help; my throat is parched. My eyes are swollen with weeping, waiting for my God to help me." Psalm 69:3, NLT), fighting the enemy ("He killed Philistines until his hand was too tired to lift his sword, and the Lord gave him a great victory that day," 2 Samuel 23:10, NLT), and criticism and persecution ("I am weary with my groaning; All night I make my bed swim; I drench my couch with my tears. My eye wastes away because of grief; it grows old because of all my enemies." Psalm 6:6-7, NKJV).[4]

I add to Swindoll's list being weary of work, our children, our spouse, or our neighbors. Many Christian's are simply tired of life. But that takes us to the third, final, and healthiest stage of discouragement: the realization that God is faithful. In 1 Kings 19, the Lord sent an angel to tend to Elijah while the prophet rested for well over a month, and then God spoke directly to Elijah to encourage him and give him direction what to do next (1 Kings 19:5-18). Nothing came of Jezebel's threat, and she later paid for her insolence against Elijah with her life (1 Kings 21:23).

> **What will help me regain my physical, spiritual, and emotional strength?**

I was reminded of God's faithfulness in the midst of fatigue dips when I saw a magazine advertisement depicting a marathon runner who was obviously in the final stages of exhaustion. Every muscle in his body appeared to be burning in pain as he rounded the last corner on the track and headed into the final stretch of his race. His right thigh and calf were bandaged from apparent injury, and he was noticeably struggling just to keep his feet churning forward. Under the photo was the caption: The Greatest Last-Place Finisher. Turned out the photo in the ad was taken during the 1968 Olympics in Mexico City, and it showed John Stephen Akhwari of Tanzania. All alone in a nearly empty stadium, he was completing the 26-mile marathon event, and he limped his way across the finish line an hour after the first-place runner had completed the race. When asked why he hadn't given up and quit running, Akhwari declared, "My country did not send me 5,000 miles to start the race," he said. "They sent me 5,000 miles to finish the race."[5]

As a follower of Christ, it's important that we finish the race that God has set before us. I'll always remember standing next to my dad's hospital bed, my hand in his, as he passed into eternity. My father was a man who lived through many years of physical pain, but he never gave up. Focused, determined, and in love with Jesus, my dad was an example of how a Christian finishes the race.

When you are faced with a fatigue dip, here are two questions you should ask yourself.

1. **What will help me regain my physical, spiritual, and emotional strength?** Sometimes you may feel like you're a hamster on a wheel, going around and around and not making much progress, or a grasshopper that is jumping but never getting anywhere. Examine what will help you recharge and then make achieving it a clear goal and pursue it intentionally.

2. **Who can I ask to help me keep a healthy balance in life?** Teams need coaches, churches need pastors, students need teachers, and you need someone to hold you accountable. I have a group that I meet with four times a year who help me keep balance in my ministry, work, and priorities. I also have

a strong, confident, loving wife who helps me in every other area of life. I need both.

Make a Bold Move: DECLUTTER your emotions.
1. You will experience different emotions as you go through each stage of the discouragement cycle.
   a. A high level of commitment, excitement and hopefulness.
   b. A feeling of exhaustion and being overwhelmed.
   c. A realization of God's faithfulness.
2. Life has seasons (Ecclesiastes 3). There is a time and season for everything under the sun. What you're experiencing is probably very normal.
3. Do the next right one thing, starting today, to declutter those things you can from your life that increase feelings of discouragement: negative entertainment, negative people, negative experiences, and negative self-talk.

How to Get Through an Emotional Dip

MOVING FORWARD WITH GOD THROUGH YOUR EMOTIONAL DIP

As I've counseled with people, I've often turned to Psalm 27. It's a powerful passage and begins with these words: "The Lord is my light and my salvation—whom shall I fear? The Lord is the stronghold of my life—of whom shall I be afraid?" In this verse, David, who had more than his share of emotional dips in his life, proclaimed that God was his light, salvation, and strength. When you align your head, heart, and hand around this truth of God's Word, you can make it through any emotional dip that comes your way. And, if you feel like you've just got to pick yourself back up and keep moving forward, Woodrow Kroll, preacher and teacher for the international Back to the Bible radio and television ministry, provided inspired counsel in his poem, "Start Over."

> **When you align your head, heart, and hand around this truth of God's Word, you can make it through any emotional dip that comes your way.**

> *When you've trusted God and walked his way*
> *When you've felt his hand lead you day by day*
> *But your steps now take you another way…*
>   *Start over.*
> *When you've made your plans and they've gone awry*
> *When you've tried your best and there's no more try*

FREEDOM FROM HIJACKED EMOTIONS

When you've failed yourself and you don't know why…
   Start over.

When you've told your friends what you plan to do
When you've trusted them and they didn't come through
   And you're all alone and it's up to you…
   Start over.

When you've failed your kids and they're grown and gone
When you've done your best but it's turned out wrong
   And now your grandchildren come along…
   Start over.

When you've prayed to God so you'll know his will
When you've prayed and prayed and you don't know still
When you want to stop cause you've had your fill…
   Start over.

When you think you're finished and want to quit
When you've bottomed out in life's deepest pit
When you've tried and tried to get out of it…
   Start over.

When the year has been long and successes few
When December comes and you're feeling blue
   God gives a January just for you…
   Start over.

Starting over means "Victories Won"
Starting over means "A Race Well Run"
Starting over means "God's Will Done"
   Don't just sit there…
   START OVER.[6]

How to Get Through an Emotional Dip

We all have times when we have to start over and trust God. Emotional dips often come like the waves of the sea and seldom with warning. The good news is you don't have to have your emotions hijacked by them. One of the reasons the Intentional Living Center exists is to lead people to a deeper and more intimate relationship with Christ amidst the complex and difficult issues and dips of life, as well as to offer hope to the discouraged.

Freedom from Hijacked Emotions

Bold Move Questions: DECLUTTER your emotions.

1. Which emotion do I wrestle with the most when I go through a dip?

_____

_____

2. How do I see God in the midst of that emotional experience?

_____

_____

3. What next right one thing can I do when facing my next emotional dip?

_____

_____

Bold Move Questions: DEVELOP a plan of action to respond to emotional triggers.

1. What practical step can I take to help me get through an invisible dip?

_____

_____

2. What do invisible dips teach me about the amount of control I have over my life?

___

3. What do others I love expect from me when they are going through an invisible dip?

___

Bold Move Questions: DECLARE who's in charge of your emotions.

1. When have I experienced Jesus reaching down into my pit to lift me out? What was that like for me?

___

2. Who is a trusted friend or counselor that I can call on when I'm in a dip? What is it about that person that caused me to think of them right now?

___

3. What is one thing I've learned while reading this book that I intend to do daily over the next 30 days to keep my heart and mind focused on today, not the mistakes of yesterday or the unknowns of tomorrow?

_____

_____

Bold Move Questions: DECLUTTER your emotions.
1. Which stage of the discouragement cycle am I in right now?
   a. A high level of commitment
   b. Feeling exhausted and overwhelmed
   c. A realization of God's faithfulness

2. What have I learned about living from each one of these three stages of discouragement?

_____

_____

3. What next right one thing can I do daily over the next 30 days to help me experience encouragement in my life?

_____

_____

7

When Words Boil Over

Good communication doesn't require a degree in counseling, but it does require more than the normal degree of patience, understanding, and empathy. In my marriage conferences, I try to reduce the complexity of communication to a simple rule: make sure that the intent behind what you say is actually what is heard. Excellence in communication reduces the kind of arguments that typically end in phrases like, "I thought you said" or "I didn't understand you to mean" or "You didn't say that," or even, "Were we in the same discussion?"

John, a listener from Idaho, called my radio show with a story that powerfully illustrated how words can affect us. As a child, John said he was repeatedly told, "You're worthless. You won't amount to anything when you grow up." He went on to share how those words became a self-fulfilling prophecy in his life as an adult. He ended up on the streets homeless and, as he put it, "without hope." He was living "down" to the level of the words that had lodged themselves in his heart as a young person. After going through a Christian rehabilitation program, John learned about God's intentional love, gave his life to Christ, and slowly started to change those memories from his childhood by intentionally reframing them with the truth of God's Word. "After I became a Christian," he said, "I was around other believers who encouraged me, and I know that God loves me and that I'm valuable to Him."

I once heard it said that, "words are the dress of thought." The words we speak are the mouthpiece of our values and beliefs, and they are a powerful instrument to either build up or tear down others in your life. One single word poorly chosen or ill-timed can change the entire course of a relationship. Careless talk or silence has done a world of hurt in many friendships and marriages. Likewise, the right words at the right time from the right people can be life changing!

Learning to use good communication takes time because it requires attention to the details. Both spoken words, and the non-verbal behavior that accompanies them, matter. In fact, the non-verbal messages often ring louder than the words that are said. Plenty of research shows that over 50 percent of human communication is non-verbal, and that statistic surely won't come as a surprise to anyone who has been married more than a week.

In a video lesson I called, "How to Read Your Mate," I reminded couples that the next right one thing they can do in their marriage is to get behind the eyes of their spouse and try to experience life as they do, reading their spouse's facial expressions, eyes, posture, and gestures in order to understand them better. We have a vocabulary to describe many common non-verbal behaviors.

- I don't like that look on your face.
- Stop rolling your eyes at me.
- Don't look so disgusted.
- You look overwhelmed.
- Please look at me when I'm speaking to you.

Words, meanwhile, draw pictures in the mind of the receiver. Some evoke images of love, affection, and understanding, others lie flat and colorless, and still others blaze with the fires of anger and hurt. Maybe that's your experience, and as a result, you feel like your spouse doesn't appreciate you, your parents don't have confidence in you, or your children don't respect you. They failed to recognize that words are powerful, and they really do mean something, good or bad, to those they love who hear them. The most effective communication happens when verbal and non-verbal expressions match.

It takes work to be a good communicator. Choosing the correct words, minding non-verbal cues, making eye contact, and then listening, reflecting, and blocking out other thoughts all require significant forethought and mental exertion. Good communication doesn't just happen. Like a river flowing downhill, communication tends to seek

> **The most effective communication happens when verbal and non-verbal expressions match.**

the lowest level unless effort is put into moving it to a high place—but the work is worth it, for Proverbs 16:24 reminds us that "gracious words are a honeycomb, sweet to the soul and healing to the bones."

Life is too short and relationships are too precious not to intentionally work on improving our communication with those we love. Let's honor the advice of Psalms 90:12 to "number our days, that we may gain a heart of wisdom" when it comes to communication.

TAKE THAT BACK

Have you ever said something to someone you love that you wish you could take back? Just like hitting the "send" button on your text or email, you immediately wish you could stop it from going out, but it's too late. You're not alone—and when you allow your words to boil over, there is great danger that the person hearing them will experience hijacked emotions. Here are a pair of examples that highlight the power of words and how they can be hurtful and damaging, even if that wasn't your intent.

Henry and Beth

"Did you have a good day at school today?" Henry asked his daughter, Beth.

"Yeah, it was okay," Beth answered. "Except that I forgot my clarinet at home, so I didn't get credit for today's class."

"What?" said Henry, frustrated.

"Dad, I was in a rush this morning, and we were running late, and..."

Henry interrupted, raising his voice. "And you can't just blow something off like that!" Then he added, "You always forget things, Beth. When are you ever going to learn to get organized?"

Sheryl and Agnes

Sheryl and her mom Agnes were out shopping when they spied an attractive outfit. "This would look great on you," Agnes said encouragingly.

"Maybe," Sheryl quipped. "But look at the price. I don't think I can afford it."

Agnes looked surprised. "Why? I thought you told me on the phone you had $80 to spend today."

"I thought I did," Sheryl responded, "but I must have made a mistake in my account. Turns out I have less to work with today than I thought."

"You never could keep track of things like that," Agnes said casually. "You never were very good at math."

Did you notice the trend in their words? Henry and Agnes both said something they shouldn't have to someone they dearly love. They may not have meant to be offensive. In fact, they probably didn't even realize they were saying anything wrong. But each one spoke words that would have been better left unsaid. They also caused hurt that, unless dealt with right away, could bring about a deeper wound that will be that much harder to heal. The unintended consequences of unthoughtful words used over an extended period of time can be profound. This is a prime example of the "I judge myself by my intentions" and "you judge me by your expectations" problem in human communication.

Make a Bold Move: DO the next right one thing.
1. Expect that even your best intentions will sometimes be misunderstood by another person.
2. Practice the next right one thing to help lessen misunderstandings when you're discussing an emotionally-charged topic with someone else.
3. Keep clarifying what you're saying until you're both clear. Doing this will improve your relationship and eliminate misunderstanding.
4. In addition to clarifying, try, if possible, to softly exit an emotionally-charged discussion with words of kindness and appreciation.

GOLDEN APPLE WORDS

For all the destructive power possessed by poorly-chosen words, those spoken appropriately are that much *more* powerful and beautiful to the hearer. One of the most-referenced Scripture verses when it comes to words is Proverbs 25:11, which says, "A word fitly spoken is like apples of gold in settings of silver." (NKJV)

In my office, on a shelf across from my desk, is a silver bowl that contains about a dozen golden-colored artificial apples. On each apple are several handwritten statements of love and affection written by marriage conference attendees from around the country. After teaching about the power of words and sharing the verse from Proverbs, I distribute several apples to the audience, asking those who want to join in to write a few words of love and respect about and to their spouse. Later in the afternoon session, I ask volunteers to share what they've written about their spouses. You can feel the atmosphere in the room lift as those encouraging words are shared. It's a high point in our marriage events. Here are just a few of the hundreds of loving statements written on those "apples of gold." They are taken from just one of the apples from the bowl in my office.

- "I would be lost without my wife."
- "I am so blessed God brought us together."
- "You're awesome."
- "You're my best friend."
- "Thank you for keeping me safe."
- "Thank you for standing with me with all we've gone through."

Here's an idea. Create your own silver bowl of golden apples in your home, write short statements of what you love, respect, and appreciate about each other on each apple, and leave the bowl in a prominent place as a reminder of your intentional love for one another.

FROM SPARK TO FLAME

The Bible's signature discourse on the power of words is James 3:3-12. Let's look at it as rendered in The Message:

"A bit in the mouth of a horse controls the whole horse. A small rudder on a huge ship in the hands of a skilled captain sets a course in the face of the strongest winds. A word out of your mouth may seem of no account, but it can accomplish nearly anything—or destroy it! It only takes a spark, remember, to set off a forest fire. A careless or wrongly placed word out of your mouth can do that. By our speech we can ruin the world, turn harmony to chaos, throw mud on a reputation, send the whole world up in smoke and go up in smoke with it, smoke right from the pit of hell. This is scary: You can tame a tiger, but you can't tame a tongue—it's never been done. The tongue runs wild, a wanton killer. With our tongues we bless God our Father; with the same tongues we curse the very men and women he made in his image. Curses and blessings out of the same mouth! My friends, this can't go on. A spring doesn't gush fresh water one day and brackish the next, does it? Apple trees don't bear strawberries, do they? Raspberry bushes don't bear apples, do they? You're not going to dip into a polluted mud hole and get a cup of clear, cool water, are you?" (TM)

It's vivid imagery, isn't it? Yet I love it because it really illustrates the impact our words have on ourselves and in the lives of others. The Word of God doesn't discount the power of words. Neither can we.

With that in mind, let's look at what I like to call my "power points" for words. These three salient principles help you understand and be aware of how to improve your communication so that you and those you love can experience life without hijacked emotions from words that hurt or damage relationships.

Power Point #1. *Choose* your words carefully

What you say and how you say it will either raise a person up or tear a person down. Humorist and lecturer Josh Billings made the statement, "There's great power in words, if you don't hitch too many of them together." He understood that it's when we say too much that we often get into trouble.

I once counseled with a couple who had been married for over 35 years. They needed help overcoming anger and learning how to forgive and improve their communication. Near the end of our first session together, the woman revealed when and how her hijacked emotion of anger toward her husband started. She locked eyes with him and said, "Twenty-five years ago, you said something about my mother, and I've never forgiven you for it." He was dumbfounded. He had no memory of the event, yet their marriage had been emotionally stuck due to a few unthoughtful words long forgotten by him but never forgotten by her.

I was speaking at a conference on the west coast when a young woman came up to me and said, "When I was in college, I ran track, and I was good at what I did. In fact, I ran faster than anyone else on the team. I set records, and my dad always came to the meets. He was firm, like a coach, and thought he was encouraging me by always saying 'You can do better'."

She continued the story. "Then I ran a race, and I broke

the state record! I ran faster than any woman in the state has ever run. I turned around to see my dad in the grandstands—and this is what he did. He had my training shoes in his hands. He threw them at me and said, 'You could have run faster'."

Now, maybe this dad's words were intended to communicate encouragement to do better, but what his daughter heard was, "You're not good enough!"

Make a Bold Move: DEVELOP a plan of action to respond to emotional triggers.

1. Be clear concerning what needs to be communicated.
2. Stay focused on the main issue, and don't get sidetracked on other less important issues.
3. Words are like pictures in the mind. Because it's impossible to know with certainty what another person is picturing in their heads, be sensitive. Pick your words for clarity and consider how they could be misunderstood.

Power Point #2. *Speak* your words carefully

Proverbs 10:19 declares, "The more talk, the less truth; the wise measure their words." (TM) I've been promising myself to write a "marital dictionary" of words that get so easily misunderstood between a husband and wife. Words can be perceived differently due to gender and age differences, life experience, faith, and several other factors.

A word like "shopping," for instance, will usually have a totally different significance to a woman than to a man.

When Words Boil Over

My wife, Donna, enjoys walking around the store looking at everything. I'm happiest when it's all over and we're on our way to the car. I'd rather shop online any day. Another word with mixed reactions is "intimacy." It may mean closeness, oneness, and sharing to one person, and sex to the other.

What you say will also have potential unintended consequences. Let's return to the earlier examples from Henry and his little girl Beth, and Agnes and her adult daughter, Sheryl. By criticizing Beth, Henry not only failed to hear out her reasoning for her mistake, he set her up to continue her forgetful behavior. By saying she "always" forgets things, he communicated a sense of inevitability to Beth; that she'll never be able to do anything right. A better response would have been for Henry to listen fully to Beth's explanation, then suggest practical ways she could not repeat the same error, perhaps by putting the clarinet by the door or with her backpack before she went to sleep so she wouldn't overlook it in the morning rush.

> **Words can be perceived differently due to gender and age differences, life experience, faith, and several other factors.**

Agnes, meanwhile, is a caring mother who loves and appreciates the time she spends with her daughter. But when she innocently brought up Sheryl's mathematical shortcomings, she awakened feelings of failure and inadequacy in Sheryl that Agnes probably didn't even know existed. There are so many people like Sheryl who can reach back to an early childhood memory of something said repeatedly by a parent, teacher, or friend that over time has torn them down emotionally. Agnes needed to pay more attention to how Sheryl reacted when she used a blanket statement like, "You never." She also needed to affirm her daughter, and let Sheryl know that she does trust and accept her as a responsible adult who is fully capable of taking care of her finances and herself.

As you get ready to speak, keep in mind the unintentional consequences that are attached to your words. Then you can make better decisions.

Make a Bold Move: DECLUTTER your emotions.

Here are three ways to avoid the unintended consequences of our words.

1. Start conversations softly. First, connect with the other person. Let them know that you care about them and want something good to come out of your conversation.
2. Ask permission before sharing something difficult. For example, say, "I have something important that I want to talk to you about. Is it okay?" By doing this, you're allowing the hearer to feel respected and able to prepare for whatever it is you are about to share.
3. Listen carefully to what they have to say to you. Respond only if you need to clarify what they said. Reflect on what they say, but don't overreact.

Power Point #3. Time your words carefully

Mark Twain said, "The right word may be effective, but no word was ever as effective as the rightly timed pause." The timing of your words is critical and, done right, can have an incredibly positive impact.

National Football League great Jerry Kramer once told this story about legendary football coach Vince Lombardi, the man for whom the Super Bowl trophy is named. "One day during the first year I played for him, he rode me unmercifully, pointing out how slow I was, how weak I was, how stupid I was. He convinced me. By the time I dragged myself into the locker room, I suspected I was the worst guard in league history. I sat in front of my locker, head down, contemplating quitting … when Lombardi came up behind me, mussed up my hair and said, 'Son, one of these days you're gonna be the greatest guard in this league.' Suddenly I was 10 feet tall, ready to do anything for him."[1]

> **Our words have the awesome power to whittle other people down to nothing or to turn them into giants capable of great things.**

Our words have the awesome power to whittle other people down to nothing or to turn them into giants capable of great things. Remember in the book of Genesis how Joseph waited until just the right time to tell his brothers who he was? He could have reacted angrily and out of spite, and he would have been perfectly justified considering what they did to him. Instead, Joseph chose to embrace his brothers with kind words. Joseph didn't reveal who he was until the time was right to result in the greatest reconciliation of their relationship.

Make a Bold Move: DEVELOP a plan of action to respond to emotional triggers.

Here are three ways to take advantage of timing.

1. Ask yourself: "Is what I'm about to say in the best interest of the other person or the best way to build the relationship?"
2. If the other person is immature, timing and content is very important.
3. Think twice, maybe three times, before you speak once.

THE POWER OF FORGIVING AND LOVING WORDS

When my children were young, I was often busy with work and mentally preoccupied whenever the family was together. One night at the dinner table when our daughter, Andrea, was about 10 years old, she tried to tell me something that was important to her, but my mind was elsewhere. Andrea was a constant chatterer as a little girl, and I tended to tune her out, which is not something I'm proud of today.

Finally, desperate to get my attention, Andrea yelled, "You never listen to me!" She then ran down the hallway to her bedroom. My first response was to get up and

When Words Boil Over

follow her down the hall while scolding her. "Young lady, you don't talk to me that way."

Yet when I got to Andrea's room and found her sobbing on her bed, God broke me. He spoke to me very clearly and guided my words as I got down on my knees next to her. "You know, Andrea, you're right. I've never been a daddy to a daughter before, and I'm learning with you. I promise to be a better listener. Will you forgive me?" Our relationship was restored and I learned a valuable lesson.

Once you realize you have said something you shouldn't, a quick and sincere apology is the best way to bring reconciliation. For many people, saying those two magic words—"I'm sorry" or "forgive me"—can be very difficult, if not impossible. Still, the Bible places a high premium on forgiveness. In His Sermon on the Mount, Jesus told of a man who was ready to offer a gift to God at the altar, but then remembered his brother had something against him. Christ said that man should be reconciled to his brother first, accomplished by apologizing and asking forgiveness for the offense. Once that was done, he could return to the altar and offer his gift (Matthew 5:23-24).

> **A great way to avoid saying things you'll later need to apologize for is to discipline yourself to get to know more about your loved ones.**

A great way to avoid saying things you'll later need to apologize for is to discipline yourself to get to know more about your loved ones. Specifically, this means discovering what motivates and encourages them, while at the same time understanding what will discourage or upset them. Good communicators speak differently to someone dealing with anxiety than they do to someone dealing with anger. An anxious person will benefit from words of comfort and reassurance, while an angry person may gain from few or no words at all. Once you truly get to know your loved ones, you'll recognize when they've been hurt by something you said. Perhaps they are quieter than usual or are just not acting right. You need to be caring and vulnerable enough to ask them if you've said something to offend them. If the answer is "yes," don't defend yourself. Simply apologize and let them know how much you love them.

> **True love reaches beyond the limitations of labels and looks at the whole person to find where their heart is.**

Remember, too, that no single word is large enough to adequately judge a person or relationship, and yet we assign words to our values, our beliefs, our thoughts, and our emotions. For instance, the word "love" is a single word that encompasses a large range of behaviors and emotions. For one person, love actually means lust; for another, friendship; and for another, companionship. The word love can symbolize a lifelong commitment, or it can simply be used to indicate something we enjoy such as food. The word "love" was so misunderstood by Christ's disciples that it took three years of ministry, the crucifixion, resurrection, and beyond before those 12 men finally began to understand what the Lord really meant by, "For God so *loved* the world." (John 3:16)

To judge your spouse or child by a single word is to miss them entirely. You may see them as being quiet, distant, or even cold. Or you may think of them as loud, obnoxious, and overbearing. Who they are as an individual is obviously much more than any of those words indicate. True love reaches beyond the limitations of labels and looks at the whole person to find where their heart is. Start by learning (perhaps again) why you love them in the first place by going deeper into who they are. This will propel you forward into avoiding wrong or unloving words and the hijacked emotions they can cause. As former British prime minister Winston Churchill so rightly said, "By swallowing evil words unsaid, no one has ever harmed his stomach."

OUR WORDS MATTER

The Bible says that we are to pray so that the words of our mouth and the meditations of our hearts are acceptable in God's sight (Psalm 19:14). The words that we speak matter. They are powerful. As you continue to develop your habits of living an intentional life in Christ, try this next right one thing: focus on speaking words of encouragement to your spouse, your children, your friends, and your co-workers. If encouragement is difficult, try not saying anything at all. That may be the next most loving thing you can do.

I once saw a study that showed that by the time the average child graduates from high school, he or she will have been criticized 16,000 times. Sad, isn't it? What those words do to the spirit of any person is destructive. Yet encouraging words bring life and hope to the hearer, and one thing is for sure: we live in a world filled with people who are desperate for encouragement. The late Cavett Robert, known as the dean of public speakers, once said, "Three billion people on the face of the earth go to bed hungry every night, but four billion people go to bed every night hungry for a simple word of encouragement and recognition."

When you are dealing with hijacked emotions and the triggers that cause them, you can respond in one of two ways. In the next chapter, we'll conclude by showing you the direction that will bring you to freedom.

> **The words that we speak matter.**

When Words Boil Over

Bold Move Questions: DO the next right one thing.

1. How do I react when my good intentioned words are misunderstood by another person?

2. What's one way I could decrease misunderstandings when discussing an emotionally-charged topic?

3. How can I make sure I use words that say what I actually intended to say?

4. What can I say to speak with kindness and appreciation when responding to someone?

Bold Move Questions: DEVELOP a plan of action to respond to emotional triggers.

Consider these three questions before you speak.

1. What really needs to be communicated?

___

2. What should I say to intentionally stay focused on the main issue?

___

3. How can I make sure my words are understood and well received?

___

Bold Move Questions: DECLUTTER your emotions.

Here are three questions to ask to avoid the unintended consequences of your words.

1. What are some phrases I can use to start a difficult conversation that will not be threatening or create a hijacked emotion?

___

2. Why would asking for permission before sharing something difficult with a loved one be helpful?

_____

_____

3. Being a good listener improves understanding in relationships. What specific thing can I do to be a better listener?

_____

_____

Bold Move Questions: DEVELOP a plan of action to respond to emotional triggers.

Here are three ways to tell if your timing is right.

1. How can I ensure what I'm about to say is in the best interest of the other person or the best way to build the relationship?"

_____

_____

2. How can I best judge if the other person is mature enough to receive what I need to say to them?

_____

_____

3. Is it the right time? How can I develop a habit of thinking twice, maybe three times, before I speak?

_____

_____

8

Intentionally Go Forward Toward Freedom

Your emotions will be your friend or your foe. They will either help you advance toward your goals or hold you back from achieving them—and when dealing with your hijacked emotions, there are only one of two ways you can respond: intentionally or unintentionally.

God's intention for how we are to live is spelled out for us by the Apostle Paul in 2 Corinthians 5:17 where he declares, "Therefore, if anyone is in Christ, the new creation has come: The old has gone, the new is here!" I liken the old and the new to wearing a coat. When we accept Jesus as our savior, we become a new person. We are given a new coat to wear as new creations in Him. But we can still choose to wear the old coat and allow the old man, our sinful nature, to rule our decisions, thoughts, and emotions. Just because we're a Christian doesn't mean that we no longer have the old coat. It's still very much present—until we choose to take it off, cast it away, and put on our new coat.

Paul then teaches in Ephesians 4:17-18, "So I tell you this, and insist on it in the Lord, that you must no longer live as the Gentiles do, in the futility of their thinking. They are darkened in their understanding and separated from the life of God because of the ignorance that is in them due to the hardening of their hearts." In essence, Paul is telling us, "Don't be like worldly people because their thinking is pointless." They are ignorant because they do not understand God and His truth. Their head, heart, and hands are all wrong because they don't know Him. Therefore, "they have given themselves over to sensuality so as to indulge in every kind of impurity, and they are full of greed." (Ephesians 4:19) They are incapable of living the good, abundant, and fulfilling life God has for them.

> **Your emotions will be your friend or your foe.**

That's not true of you. As a Christian, you can live intentionally in grateful response to God's grace (Ephesians 2:8-9) to His glory and your benefit. With your new life in Christ, you can choose to respond to your emotions in a way that will conform you to Christ and provide motivation to grow in Him.

CHALLENGE YOUR ASSUMPTIONS

Assumptions are anything without proof that you believe to be true about yourself, others, and the world. If you assume the worst, then it's not surprising that your emotions will be easily hijacked whenever things aren't going as you hoped. If you want to become an intentional person, the first thing you have to do is challenge every one of your assumptions. When what you say you believe aligns with what you assume, your emotional life is more easily managed. However, if what you say you believe doesn't align with your assumptions, your emotions can be easily hijacked.

- If you say you believe God made you, but you assume your life has no purpose, your hijacked emotion is discouragement.
- If you say you believe God has a plan for your life, but you assume you're not capable, your hijacked emotion is discouragement as you compare yourself to others.
- If you say you believe God is in charge, but you need to control everything, your hijacked emotion is worry.
- If you say you believe God saved you, but you assume you don't measure up, your hijacked emotion is fear of rejection.
- If you say you believe God loves you, but you assume you're not lovable, your hijacked emotion is loneliness.

People who are unintentional are led by their assumptions. I know assumptions have gotten me into trouble more often than I'd like to admit. I recall when Donna asked me to trim one of the trees in our yard. "It's overtaking our driveway," she pointed out. I was in the middle of another project that at the time felt important, and I assumed that she meant for me to drop what I was I doing right there and then. So, instead of maturely clarifying her desired timetable for the trimming, I petulantly responded, "Fine. I'll get right to it!" That, as you'd imagine, led to a brief but poignant exchange between us that set straight my wrong assumption—and led to an apology from me.

> **Over the next 30 days, *do* the next right one thing to better your life and *stop* doing one thing that is holding you back.**

It's common to make assumptions. After all, clarifying every word or action from another person is impractical and exhausting. The problem isn't the assumptions you get right. It's the ones you get wrong that often lead to someone having a hijacked emotion. In addition, many people exist at a level of mediocrity in their lives because they've made wrong assumptions about themselves that limit their potential when there is no limit to what we can do with God's help. Nothing is impossible for Him.

A great way to start living intentionally by making right assumptions and creating new habits for your life is to take my 30-day challenge. Over the next 30 days, *do* the next right one thing to better your life and *stop* doing one thing that is holding you back. (See the encouraging verses in the appendix that remind you of who you are in Christ. Memorize some of them as part of your 30-day challenge.)

Make a Bold Move: DECIDE who's in charge of your emotions.

1. Because of God's intentional love for you, challenge your negative assumptions about yourself.
2. Because of God's intentional love for other people, challenge your negative assumptions about others in your life.
3. Because God's in charge of the future, challenge your negative assumptions whenever you think about the future.

TAKE RESPONSIBILITY AND FIND SOLUTIONS

Intentional people take personal responsibility and are willing to say, "I am one hundred percent responsible for what I do and what I don't do." In today's culture, it's common to blame everybody else for what is wrong in life. It is far better to simply take ownership of what you can and to proactively deal with the issues you face.

I recently talked with a man who had lost his job due to anger. He blamed his misfortune on his boss, the human resources department, and his direct supervisor. He attempted to convince everybody, and probably himself, that the problem wasn't with him, it was with others. His failure to recognize and confront the root issues of his anger not only cost him his job, but his marriage was on the brink because he wouldn't respond to his hijacked emotions.

A great question to ask yourself is, "How did I contribute to the issue that has led to how I'm feeling right now?" That causes you to take responsibility and then focus on the solution instead of the problem. I've always exhorted my ministry team, "Please don't bring me a problem without also presenting at least two ways of solving it." Anybody can see problems, but it requires a solution-focused person to help solve them. Solution-focused people are confident and forward looking. They look at the facts, and instead of denying their feelings, they use their emotions to spur themselves to action. They experience their emotions, but they are not directed by them. They don't allow themselves to be hijacked.

> **Intentional people take personal responsibility and are willing to say, "I am one hundred percent responsible for what I do and what I don't do."**

Julia was a problem-focused person. When she called my show, she was quick to share a long list of what was wrong in her marriage. "He doesn't put his things away at night." "He ignores me when I ask him questions." "He yells at the kids too much." "I can't count on him to show up when he says he will." "He's always forgetting to pay the bills on time." She ended by saying, "I'm so angry and frustrated with him, but I don't

Intentionally Go Forward Toward Freedom

know what to do!" Julia's concerns are legitimate and should be addressed to help their marriage. The problem isn't that she has complaints. The problem is she didn't take action to create forward motion toward addressing the problems. It's not that she can solve her husband's problems; he has to take responsibility for those. But she can take back control of her hijacked emotions of frustration and anger by practicing active respect, which I introduced in Chapter 1 and is featured in my book *Starved for Affection*. The chapter is entitled, "Overcoming Roadblocks Through Active Respect," and it lists the benefits of active respect as follows:

- It's proactive. It eliminates the feeling of throwing up your hands and asking, "What can I do?"
- It gets you off the hook. It may be that you want to stay on the hook because you're more of the problem than you'd like to honestly admit.
- It allows your spouse to face himself. Whenever we get in the way of someone truly seeing himself for who he is—his attitudes, beliefs, and behaviors—we provide a way of escape or avoidance and keep him from truly understanding what needs to be changed.
- It helps you lower your frustration level and reduces feelings of guilt and anger. By putting the responsibility in its rightful place, you unburden yourself from an unnecessary weight.[1]

There are three keys to success in using active respect.

Freedom from Hijacked Emotions

1. **Focus only on the present behavior and attitude.** Focusing too far into the past, or using general statements of frustration, is often only a diversion from facing the issues right in front of you. Julia, for instance, was guilty of generalizing her frustration. A solutions-focused approach is to focus on what's happening today, not what occurred two months ago.
2. **Clearly express your needs, desires and wants.** This may be difficult for pleaser-type personalities, but you can confront issues that have hijacked your emotions without being confrontational. Julia could have said to her husband, "Honey, when I opened the mail today, I found another late notice on our mortgage payment. I checked, and it's negatively impacted our credit score. We've been charged hundreds of dollars in late fees. It's important to me that we keep our bills current and get our credit score up. I'd like to help by going over our bills each month with you." In this scenario, Julia clearly expressed her needs (to keep the bills current), her desires (to have a good credit score), and her wants (to help to make sure it gets done). Julia moved from problems to solutions and from hijacked emotions to action.
3. **Keep the ball on your spouse's side of the net.** This is the part of love that can be tough—literally. Active respect is willing to hold the person you love accountable for their behavior and attitude. Let's say Julia's husband pushed back against her offer of help with the family finances. She could then

respond with, "Okay, I'll leave it to you—as long as you keep everything current." If he changes his behavior, that's great. But if he doesn't, Julia will need to be intentionally bold enough to insist on getting involved.

Make a Bold Move: DEVELOP a plan of action to respond to emotional triggers.
1. Think about one important relationship in your life that needs to be addressed.
2. Rehearse the words you could use to most effectively express your needs, desires, and wants concerning the behavior in that relationship.
3. Keep the ball of responsibility in their court.

TAKE BOLD A-C-T-I-O-N

The line between mediocrity and accomplishment is action. Jesus commanded action. After healing the leper in Luke 5:12-15, he told the man to go show himself to the priest. When the lawyer asked Christ in Luke 10:25-28 what was required to inherit eternal life, Jesus told him and then said, "Do this and you will live." In the parable of the Good Samaritan that followed, Christ called His listeners to action.

If you want freedom from hijacked emotions, you need to be bold. That's why I included all of the Bold Move actions throughout this book. Let's take a quick look at each letter in the word "action" to break this down a bit further.

Freedom from Hijacked Emotions

A = Act by stepping out in faith. When you do, you will likely fall down at first. That's okay. Just get back up and keep going.

C = Confidently go forward. A Norwegian proverb says, "a hero is one who knows how to hang on one minute longer." Confidence helps you to stay with something just a little longer than the next person. Confidence is courage in action. It's not that you lack fear, but that you have the willingness to push through in spite of it. You'll lose your confidence when you lack faith, knowledge, healthy relationships, sleep, adequate resources, trust, or clarity. But you'll gain and strengthen your confidence to move forward as you grow in your faith in Christ, gain knowledge of His Word, build healthy relationships, get plenty of rest, acquire adequate resources, decide to trust God, and think clearly.

> The line between mediocrity and accomplishment is action.

T = Time your action correctly. In order to succeed going forward, you need to know when to act and be willing to wait, if needed, until the time is right.

I = Imaginatively proceed. God gave you an imagination so you can see things that don't exist today but could happen in the future. Imagination will help you rehearse managing your emotions intentionally, and it will give you hope that things will get better.

O = Overtly act for all to see. Declare what you need to do to respond intentionally to emotional triggers, and

Intentionally Go Forward Toward Freedom

then encourage trusted family and friends to hold you accountable to your commitments.

N = Never look back! The rearview mirror in your car is small compared to your windshield because safe driving requires spending more time looking forward than looking back. As you keep your focus in front of you, it will strengthen you through times of difficulty and defeat, and help you look at the big picture.

Make a Bold Move: DECLUTTER your emotions.
1. Build your faith in order to boldly step out and experience freedom from a hijacked emotion.
2. Be intentional about when you address emotionally-loaded topics with other people.
3. Imagine the freedom you will experience from your hijacked emotions as you declutter them from your life.

DO THE NEXT RIGHT ONE THING

If you really want to live a relationally, physically, spiritually, and *emotionally* healthy life, you need to stop doing more of the same thing day after day that *isn't* working now and start doing the next right one thing. Several years ago, I developed a "One Thing" wristband that I wear every day. Thousands have requested their own "One Thing" wristband as a daily reminder to do the next right one thing for God's glory. Each morning as I put the band on my wrist, I quietly ask God to help me focus on the next right one thing that is most beneficial for that day that will bring Him glory and the most benefit to my life.

In *The Power of One Thing*, I wrote about how doing the next right one thing in nine areas of life can change everything:

- The power of one thing will change your thinking.
- The power of one thing will change your attitude.
- The power of one thing will change your emotions.
- The power of one thing will change your words.
- The power of one thing will change how you use time.
- The power of one thing will change how you pick friends.
- The power of one thing will unclutter your life.
- The power of one thing will change the questions you ask.
- The power of one thing will change how you make decisions.[2]

Notice how each of these nine areas require intentionality with thinking, emotions, and behavior: your head, heart, and hands. Living intentionally in each of these nine areas will help you grow in confidence in your faith and live the way you want to become in Christ.

If you want to grow spiritually, you have to do the things that will help you grow. Here are 10 next right one things that will give your spiritual life a boost and cause you to live in freedom from hijacked emotions.

1. **Pray.** Prayer is your powerful opportunity to commune with the living God and is a beautiful invitation to draw close to Christ. Take time daily

Intentionally Go Forward Toward Freedom

to bring your needs and struggles to Him. He will hear and respond.
2. **Meditate.** In the quietness, away from family and television and other distractions, meditate on key passages of the Bible or consider a truth that you heard at a recent church service. Ask the Holy Spirit to reveal Himself to you.
3. **Memorize Scripture.** When you are faced with a challenge or decision, you need to be equipped with the Word of God to know how to respond biblically. Place verses on your iPad, your phone, or a Post-it Note. Put it wherever you'll see it. Then read it over and over until you memorize it.

> **If you want to grow spiritually, you have to do the things that will help you grow.**

4. **Serve others.** You might have a neighbor or coworker who is going through a difficult time. Take them something to eat, give them a word of encouragement, or go and wash their car or clean their yard. Find opportunities to love others.
5. **Share.** You glorify God simply by sharing the reality of what God has done in your life. Tell others, and do it often.
6. **Worship.** This is not only a Sunday church activity. You can worship God when you're driving down the street, as you clean your house, or as you do other errands. Worship occurs when you praise Him, and you can do that anywhere, anytime.

7. **Tithe.** Giving God 10 percent of your income is an act of worship and obedience that shows your trust in Him to provide for all of your needs.
8. **Read.** There are many great biographies or autobiographies of Christians like D.L. Moody, John and Charles Wesley, and many others. These men and women lived through trials and difficulties, and their stories are shining examples of growing faith.
9. **Listen to Christian radio.** Turn off the negative influences of the outside world and tune in to the hope coming through the songs and scriptures on Christian radio. Allow the music and the programming to become a soundtrack for your home.
10. **Be active in your church.** The Bible says, "Let us consider how we may spur one another on toward love and good deeds, not giving up meeting together, as some are in the habit of doing, but encouraging one another." (Hebrews 10:24-25) There are no perfect people, no perfect churches, or no perfect pastors, but get involved in a church where the Bible is accurately taught and emphasized.[3]

Intentionally Go Forward Toward Freedom

Bold Move Questions: DECIDE who's in charge of your emotions.

1. What is one assumption about yourself that needs to change for the better?

_____

_____

2. What is one assumption about others that needs to change for the better?

_____

_____

3. What is one assumption about the future that needs to change for the better?

_____

_____

Bold Move Questions: DEVELOP a plan of action to respond to emotional triggers.

1. What is one present issue in an important relationship that needs to be addressed?

_____

_____

2. What words could you use to most effectively express your needs, desires, and wants concerning that issue?

_____

_____

3. What do you need to do in order to keep the ball of responsibility in their court?

_____

_____

Bold Move Questions: DECLUTTER your emotions.

Think about the person from the previous Make a Bold Move section and answer these questions:

1. What will help you build your faith in order to boldly step out to experience freedom from a hijacked emotion?

_____

_____

2. When is the best time to step out in faith and act? If not now, when? If never, why?

_____

_____

Intentionally Go Forward Toward Freedom

3. What does it feel like whenever you imagine having freedom from your hijacked emotions?

_____

_____

One More Thing

If you're like me, your morning ritual is to mentally rehearse your plans for the day. Maybe your "to do list" is typically unrealistically long and unattainable, eventually resulting in it being set aside and ignored. I call this the "good intentioned life," packed with lots of good intentions but without consistent follow through that usually leads to procrastination and discouragement. The other extreme is the "unintentional life." Much like a grasshopper, you jump from one thing to another every day as you face threats, challenges, opportunities, or perhaps even boredom.

Both extremes will result in mediocrity with weariness and frustration by day's end. You'll tell yourself, "Tomorrow, I'll do things differently." The sun comes up, your energy is restored, and yesterday's commitments are only a memory. But, if you're not careful, you'll simply repeat the unhealthy emotional patterns from the day before—similar to what Bill Murray's character did in the 1993 comedy movie, *Groundhog Day*. Living the same day over and over without emotional growth is frustrating and confining. Therefore, resist the gravitational pull back toward your "good intentioned" or "unintentional" life of yesterday. Both will lead to regrets and some form of hijacked emotions. Instead, live an intentional life in Christ. It's the path to overcoming any hijacked emotion.

You may be the type of person who highlights every good idea you read. Perhaps you have felt overwhelmed while reading, thinking, *This is all too much for me to do. I've tried things before and it's not for me.* Maybe you have skimmed through the book and landed here on "One More Thing," hoping I'll summarize everything for you in a couple of pages and save you a lot of time. I admit I've done that myself! So, here it is in one sentence:

You will become tomorrow whatever you intentionally think, feel, and do today!

Our mission at the Intentional Living Center is to help people turn good intentions into a permanent reality for God's glory and their benefit. Finding freedom from hijacked emotions is a marathon, not a sprint. Doing nothing means nothing will change. Doing everything will lead to fatigue and discouragement. It's time to allow God, through intentional living, to change your emotional destiny so that you can get off the current path that keeps you in the cul-de-sac of old patterns of thinking, feeling, and reacting. In *The Power of One Thing*, I shared what that pattern looks like:

Step 1: I need to change.
Step 2: I want to change.

Step 3: I commit to change.
Step 4: I try to change.
Step 5: I meet resistance to change.
Step 6: I stop changing and go back to what I was doing before.
Step 7: I feel discouraged because I didn't change and my commitment is gone – until I start the cycle all over again.[1]

Break the pattern by being intentional with your life! Do the next right one thing until it becomes a habit for life. Don't attempt to do everything, but do start today by doing the next right one thing. Make it your 30-day challenge to allow God to empower you to act. Don't live a good intentioned life with its regrets or the unintentional life with its fatigue. Don't allow family, friends, work, or especially yourself to hold you back, pull you down, or discourage you with lies. Go the distance until you've experienced freedom from your hijacked emotions.

If you are one that skipped to the end of the book, I encourage you to return to the beginning and start to unlock the strategies behind finding freedom from hijacked emotions by living intentionally in Christ. You *can* do it!

Join the Intentional Living journey and share what God is doing in your life. There are archives of past radio shows and podcasts, many free resources, and lots of helpful information available right now at our website: www.theintentionallife.com.

Appendix

Here are several Bible verses that will encourage you and lead to freedom over hijacked emotions.

Loneliness

Deuteronomy 31:8 – The Lord himself goes before you and will be with you; he will never leave you nor forsake you. Do not be afraid; do not be discouraged.

Isaiah 41:10 – So do not fear, for I am with you; do not be dismayed, for I am your God. I will strengthen you and help you; I will uphold you with my righteous right hand.

Psalm 34:7 – The angel of the Lord encamps around those who fear him, and he delivers them.

Proverbs 18:24 – One who has unreliable friends soon comes to ruin, but there is a friend who sticks closer than a brother.

Depression

2 Samuel 22:2-3 – He said: "The Lord is my rock, my fortress and my deliverer; my God is my rock, in whom I take refuge, my shield and the horn of my salvation. He is my stronghold, my refuge and my savior—from violent people you save me."

Psalm 34:18 – The Lord is close to the brokenhearted and saves those who are crushed in spirit.

Psalm 40:1, 3-4 – I waited patiently for the Lord; he turned to me and heard my cry ... He put a new song in my mouth, a hymn of praise to our God. Many will see and fear the Lord and put their trust in him. Blessed is the one who trusts in the Lord, who does not look to the proud, to those who turn aside to false gods.

Psalm 42:11 – Why, my soul, are you downcast? Why so disturbed within me? Put your hope in God, for I will yet praise him, my Savior and my God.

Psalm 55:22 – Cast your cares on the Lord and he will sustain you; he will never let the righteous be shaken.

Psalm 116:8 – For you, Lord, have delivered me from death, my eyes from tears, my feet from stumbling.

2 Corinthians 1:3-4 – Praise be to the God and Father of our Lord Jesus Christ, the Father of compassion and the God of all comfort, who comforts us in all our troubles, so that we can comfort those in any trouble with the comfort we ourselves receive from God.

Appendix

James 1:2-4 – Consider it pure joy, my brothers and sisters, whenever you face trials of many kinds, because you know that the testing of your faith produces perseverance. Let perseverance finish its work so that you may be mature and complete, not lacking anything.

Fear, Worry and Anxiety

Psalm 34:4 – I sought the Lord, and he answered me; he delivered me from all my fears.

Psalm 46:10 – He says, "Be still, and know that I am God; I will be exalted among the nations, I will be exalted in the earth."

Psalm 112:7-8 – They will have no fear of bad news; their hearts are steadfast, trusting in the Lord. Their hearts are secure, they will have no fear; in the end they will look in triumph on their foes.

Proverbs 12:25 – Anxiety weighs down the heart, but a kind word cheers it up.

Matthew 6:25 – Therefore I tell you, do not worry about your life, what you will eat or drink; or about your body, what you will wear. Is not life more than food, and the body more than clothes?

Luke 12:29-31 – And do not set your heart on what you will eat or drink; do not worry about it. For the pagan world runs after all such things, and your Father knows that you need them. But seek his kingdom, and these things will be given to you as well.

Philippians 4:6-8 – Do not be anxious about anything, but in every situation, by prayer and petition, with thanksgiving, present your requests to God. And the peace of God, which transcends all understanding, will guard your hearts and your minds in Christ Jesus. Finally, brothers and sisters, whatever is true, whatever is noble, whatever is right, whatever is pure, whatever is lovely, whatever is admirable—if anything is excellent or praiseworthy—think about such things.

2 Timothy 1:7 – For the Spirit God gave us does not make us timid, but gives us power, love and self-discipline.

Anger

Psalm 37:8 – Refrain from anger and turn from wrath; do not fret—it leads only to evil.

Proverbs 14:29 – Whoever is patient has great understanding, but one who is quick-tempered displays folly.

Proverbs 15:1 – A gentle answer turns away wrath, but a harsh word stirs up anger.

Proverbs 15:18 – A hot-tempered person stirs up conflict, but the one who is patient calms a quarrel.

Proverbs 19:11 – A person's wisdom yields patience; it is to one's glory to overlook an offense.

Appendix

Proverbs 29:11 – Fools give full vent to their rage, but the wise bring calm in the end.

Ecclesiastes 7:9 – Do not be quickly provoked in your spirit, for anger resides in the lap of fools.

Matthew 5:22 – But I tell you that anyone who is angry with a brother or sister will be subject to judgment. Again, anyone who says to a brother or sister, "Raca," is answerable to the court. And anyone who says, "You fool!" will be in danger of the fire of hell.

Ephesians 4:26 – "In your anger do not sin": Do not let the sun go down while you are still angry.

Colossians 3:8 – But now you must also rid yourselves of all such things as these: anger, rage, malice, slander, and filthy language from your lips.

James 1:19-20 – My dear brothers and sisters, take note of this: Everyone should be quick to listen, slow to speak and slow to become angry, because human anger does not produce the righteousness that God desires.

Peace

Isaiah 26:3 – You will keep in perfect peace those whose minds are steadfast, because they trust in you.

Matthew 11:28-30 – Come to me, all you who are weary and burdened, and I will give you rest. Take my yoke upon you and learn from me, for I am gentle and humble in heart, and you will find rest for your souls. For my yoke is easy and my burden is light.

John 14:27 – Peace I leave with you; my peace I give you. I do not give to you as the world gives. Do not let your hearts be troubled and do not be afraid.

John 16:33 – I have told you these things, so that in me you may have peace. In this world you will have trouble. But take heart! I have overcome the world.

Romans 12:18 – If it is possible, as far as it depends on you, live at peace with everyone.

Romans 14:19 – Let us therefore make every effort to do what leads to peace and to mutual edification.

Galatians 5:22-23 – But the fruit of the Spirit is love, joy, peace, forbearance, kindness, goodness, faithfulness, gentleness and self-control. Against such things there is no law.

Colossians 3:15 – Let the peace of Christ rule in your hearts, since as members of one body you were called to peace. And be thankful.

Philippians 4:9 – Whatever you have learned or received or heard from me, or seen in me—put it into practice. And the God of peace will be with you.

1 Peter 5:7 – Cast all your anxiety on him because he cares for you.

Bibliography

You Can Live Free

[1] Dr. Randy Carlson, *The Power of One Thing*, Tyndale Momentum, 2009, p. 9.

Chapter One

[1] Dr. Randy Carlson, *Starved for Affection*, Tyndale House Publishers, Inc., 2005, p. 131.
[2] Dr. Randy Carlson, *Father Memories*, Moody Press, 1992, p. 13.
[3] https://news.gallup.com/poll/249098/americans-stress-worry-anger-intensified-2018.aspx

Chapter Three

[1] http://www.dictionary-quotes.com/one-of-lifes-primal-situations-the-game-of-hide-and-seek-oh-the-delicious-thrill-of-hiding-while-the-others-come-looking-for-you-the-delicious-terror-of-being-discovered-but-what-panic-wh/?amp

Freedom from Hijacked Emotions

Chapter Four

[1] Charles Duhigg, *The Power of Habit*, Random House Publishing, 2012, p. xvii

Chapter Five

[1] Dr. Randy Carlson, *Starved for Affection*, Tyndale House Publishers, Inc., 2005, p. 13.

[2] Dr. Randy Carlson, *Starved for Affection*, Tyndale House Publishers, Inc., 2005, p. 15.

[3] Dr. Randy Carlson, *The Power of One Thing*, Tyndale Momentum, 2009, p. 47-51.

Chapter Six

[1] Doris Kearns Goodwin, *Team of Rivals: The Political Genius of Abraham Lincoln*, Simon & Schuster, 2005, p. 51.

[2] Ibid.

[3] Dr. Randy Carlson, *Father Memories*, Moody Press, 1992, p. 185-186.

[4] Charles R. Swindoll, *Growing Strong in the Seasons of Life*, Multnomah Press, 1983, p. 136.

[5] https://www.olympic.org/news/marathon-man-akhwari-demonstrates-super-human-spirit.

[6] Woodrow Kroll, "Start Over," http://www.turnbacktogod.com/poem-start-over/

Chapter Seven

[1] Jerry Kramer, "Winning Isn't Everything," New York Times, January 24, 1997, A17.

Chapter Eight

[1] Dr. Randy Carlson, *Starved for Affection*, Tyndale House Publishers, Inc., 2005, p. 133-134.

Bibliography

[2] Dr. Randy Carlson, *The Power of One Thing*, Tyndale Momentum, 2009, p. xvi.

[3] From the list, "InTENtional for Growing Spiritually." Copyright 2016 by Dr. Randy Carlson.

One More Thing

[1] Dr. Randy Carlson, *The Power of One Thing*, Tyndale Momentum, 2009, p. 15.

What if **ONE THING** could change everything?

THE
POWER
OF
ONE
THING

How to Intentionally Change Your Life

DR. RANDY CARLSON

Dr. Randy Carlson invites you to begin moving toward change one daily, intentional step at a time in **The Power of One Thing**.

IntentionalLiving™ PRESS

Why We Crave It, How to Get It, and Why It's so Important in Marriage

STARVED for AFFECTION

Why we crave it, how to get it, and why it's so important in marriage

DR. RANDY CARLSON

Dr. Randy Carlson teaches why affection is so important and how to develop that essential, active ingredient in marriage

IntentionalLiving™ PRESS

Want to Go Deeper?

Become a Member of the Intentional Living Center!

Become a member of the Intentional Living Center today with your ongoing monthly donation and receive brand new mentoring content every month, absolutely free!

Dr. Randy will be your personal coach on CD with practical help on issues you face.

IntentionalLiving™ — PRESS —

When it comes to parenting, marriage and relationships, people are turning to best-selling author, counselor and radio personality Dr. Randy Carlson. Dr. Randy hosts Intentional Living, a live call-in program syndicated to radio stations nationwide.

TheIntentionalLife.com

You can find a list of the ways to listen or subscribe to the *Intentional Living* Podcast online at theintentionallife.com

IntentionalLiving™ PRESS